TURFGRASS SOD PRODUCTION

The author is Stephen T. Cockerham,
Superintendent of Agricultural Operations for the
University of California, Riverside.

For information about ordering this publication, write to:

Publications
Division of Agriculture and Natural Resources
University of California
6701 San Pablo Avenue
Oakland, California 94608-1239

or telephone (415) 642-2431

Publication 21451

ISBN 0-931876-85-0
Library of Congress No. 88-71015

Printed in the United States of America.

To simplify information, trade names of products have been used. No endorsement of named products is intended, nor is criticism implied of similar products which are not mentioned.

Production: Jim Coats, *Senior Editor;*
Franz Baumhackl, *Senior Artist.*

Issued in furtherance of Cooperative Extension work, Acts of May 8 and June 30, 1914, in cooperation with the U.S. Department of Agriculture.
Kenneth R. Farrell, Director of Cooperative Extension, University of California.

1m-pr-6/88-WJC/FB

Contents

Tables

Acknowledgments

This project would not have been completed without the support and encouragement of Vic Gibeault, Dick Baldwin, Steve McLaughlin, and John Van Dam. My wife Barbara was particularly important in helping make it happen. Many colleagues in the sod business have been my teachers over the years. Tobias Grether stands out as the most significant. He founded the sod industry in California and taught many young people what sod production was all about. John Scherer, Dave Knutson, and Dave Barlow were important contributors to the experience of sod farm ownership. The members and executives of the American Sod Producers Association have been a tremendous resource of friendship and learning, especially Bill Campbell, Ike Thomas, Bob Garey, Harry Bacon, Walt Pemrick, Ray Johnson, Al Gardner, and John Addink. Above all, my parents have made the successes and failures of being in the sod business worthwhile.

Stephen T. Cockerham

Dedication

To Garrett Charles Cockerham (1968–1985).
He loved everything about the sod farm.
He wanted me to write it all down someday.

1
Background and History

This publication has been written with three groups in mind: new employees of an established company, turfgrass management students, and individuals thinking of going into the sod business. Commercial sod production is an extremely complex business. Members of all three groups need to know what is involved.

Sod companies, with rare exceptions, are owned and operated by entrepreneurs. The structure, culture, and philosophy vary a great deal from company to company, so depicting a typical sod operation is difficult. For this reason, I will describe sod production through a hypothetical turfgrass sod company called *Eucre Sod* ("Eucre" is the way one might pronounce the abbreviation UCR, for the University of California at Riverside).

Eucre Sod is organized in the functional divisions of Administration, Sales, Production, and Distribution. Administration is the front office and general management. The sales division markets and services the product, the production division grows and harvests the crop, and the distribution division gets the product to the customer. The administration division keeps the other three divisions working well together and keeps the company solvent.

Besides its own form of management, each sod company has unique soils, equipment, water resources, and climatic conditions. Eucre Sod is actually a blend of several companies with different circumstances. Where Eucre Sod follows a particular method or technique, remember that the situation is hypothetical and that the practice should not be considered a general recommendation.

Turfgrass sod production is often compared to turfgrass management, and just as frequently compared to general agriculture and to manufacturing. It is similar to, yet unlike, all three.

Whereas turfgrass management focuses upon the aesthetics and playability of a turf sward, sod production puts the priority on a product that can be marketed to a consumer. Where general agriculture focuses upon getting a crop to market in its harvest season, sod production harvests over a long period, even year-round in the sun belt. Manufacturing focuses upon efficiently turning raw materials into a product, regardless of external influences, but sod production adds the variables of the environment and a living plant.

A new industry

The turfgrass sod industry in the United States started on the East Coast in the early 1920s. Pastures of native grasses, mostly Kentucky bluegrass, were mowed short by entrepreneurial farmers and made to look somewhat like a lawn. The sod was cut and lifted with spades, and then sold, at first for use on golf courses. Even though gardeners in Europe and the United States had long lifted and transplanted turfgrass sod, it was the Americans who developed it into a commercial product. As the business grew, turfgrass producers introduced horse-drawn sod cutters. By the 1930s, the home lawn was the predominant end product, and sod production had spread to the upper Midwest, especially in Michigan and around Chicago, Illinois.

In the late 1940s, the self-propelled sod cutter brought with it a more efficient way to harvest a sod pad cut to uniform thickness. Improved disease-resistant selections of Kentucky bluegrass were introduced in the 1950s, and so began the era of "cultured sod" as opposed to pasture sod. Very little pasture sod reaches the U.S. market today—nearly all turfgrass sod is cultured.

The 1970s saw several major advances in sod production technology. By far the most important was the development of the sod harvester, which allowed two or three workers to perform the work of 20 to 30. Plastic netting laid at the soil line stabilized the mat and root structure and cut the crop maturity time by up to 75 percent. Developments in

This wide expanse of uniform turf is ready for harvest.

plant nutrition and weed, disease, and insect control caused a tremendous increase in the uniformity, rooting ability, and general quality of the turfgrass sod. New marketing techniques that were developed or adapted from other industries, and large self-propelled rotary mowers, wide vacuums and sweepers, totable forklifts, and hydraulically driven reels on reel mowers all came to the sod industry in this decade.

In 1982, 43 of the 50 states produced sod, and sales were estimated at $360 million. Turfgrass sod was available in every major city in the United States and in some not-so-major towns.

Turfgrass sod is perishable and very heavy. The product has a shelf life of only 36 hours or so, and heavy-duty equipment must be used for its transport. The production facility must also be close to the market. Because of these requirements, sod production has developed around large cities. Unfortunately, land is expensive near big cities, and this has kept the cost of entering the sod business high.

Growing turfgrasses is a constant learning process. New technologies develop with incredible speed. Diseases, weeds, and other pests seem uncanny in their ability to keep ahead of the grower. Economic trends and business cycles change constantly. The sod producer must work hard just to keep up.

Educational seminars, meetings, and expositions are valuable sources of up-to-date information, and sod grower associations can be useful for any producer, whether new to the enterprise or experienced. The American Sod Producers Association has nationwide membership, and growers in many states have their own associations. The successful sod producer is ever alert for any opportunity to learn.

California

The sod industry in California began production in 1958, and by 1986 it had grown to an estimated 7,000 acres, with annual sales estimated at 4,600 acres and $40 million. The industry in California was relatively independent of economic cycles until the early 1980s. There were few growers, and although they competed for some large or prestigious orders, the market was growing faster that the supply.

When the economy was booming, as it was most of the time, sod sales were good and the annual growth was predictable in correlation with housing starts. During economic downturns, sod sales continued as if nothing had happened—the correlation with housing starts no longer held. In good times, it seemed, homes sold quickly and the new homeowners purchased sod, whereas in slow times the developers bought sod to increase the attractiveness of the unsold homes.

In the mid-1970s the few existing large California sod companies were challenged by several new, small sod companies. Even so, there was plenty of business to go around. Then in 1979, when the California sod industry was recovering from a severe 3-year statewide drought and what was arguably the most serious energy crisis in history, the U.S. economy began to turn sour.

Interest rates climbed at an incredible pace. This brought the housing industry to a stop and forced the sod growers to use a very large portion of their cash flow to service their debts. Accounts receivable became extremely difficult to collect, and inflation forced supply and labor costs to increase dramatically. The fun went out of sod production.

As can be expected when sales become tight, the long-stable price structure began to disintegrate. In California, the large growers began to cut prices. At first only those with extensive investor financial resources offered lower rates. The other large growers soon followed, and then all producers joined in, causing chaos in the market.

From 1979 through 1983, the state suffered the worst economic recession since the collapse of 1929. It was certainly the worst in the history of the sod industry. A classic shake-out occurred. Large growers acquired smaller growers and got larger. No California sod company is known to have been forced into bankruptcy, but all struggled, some more than others. In 1987, out of a total of 49 growers, fewer than half-a-dozen companies controlled an estimated two-thirds of the statewide market.

In 1983 and 1984, the sod market began to stabilize again, but it was a very different sod industry than was known before the recession. The tie to the housing industry was unmistakable, and the sod market became subject to the vagaries of that industry. The market became much more difficult for a new grower to penetrate, and became much less attractive to investors.

The California sod market still holds vast opportunities because of the state's rapid population growth, but any grower who hopes to succeed will have to combine good business decisions, a thorough understanding of the market, and a very efficient operation. Overproduction, not a consideration prior to 1979, could become a real threat to the industry in the late 1980s and 1990s.

2
Administration

Eucre Sod

The administration division of Eucre Sod consists of the general manager, order clerk, and part-time bookkeeper. Besides overseeing the company finances and operations, the general manager's work includes planning, budgeting, managing credit, and purchasing. The order clerk answers the telephone, takes customer orders, coordinates sod harvest with orders, dispatches deliveries, prepares invoices, and receives visitors. The bookkeeper works half days and keeps the records of accounts receivable and accounts payable, bills the customers, pays the suppliers, keeps the payroll records, and prepares the payroll.

The effort required for most of the jobs of general management is pretty well accepted. However, purchasing is usually not thought of as particularly significant. In companies the size of Eucre Sod, the general manager spends a great deal of time as the purchasing agent. Time is required for talking to supplier sales representatives who call on the company, getting competitive prices, checking orders upon delivery, and expediting orders. Often, the general manager must spend many hours just trying to locate a needed part.

Planning and budgeting are also critical, time-consuming jobs of the general manager. Information for planning and budget decisions comes from other company personnel, especially the sales and production staffs.

Order processing

Customers buy sod over the telephone. It is not unusual for the order taker to develop a rapport with the regular customers. The telephone personality of the order taker can be a valuable sales tool.

At Eucre Sod, the order is recorded by customer name, type of turfgrass, quantity, terms of purchase (credit, COD, etc.), date of delivery, delivery address, and the nearest major cross street. The completed order form is given to the trucking dispatcher to use in routing the delivery on the day required. The type of turfgrass, quantity, and order number are posted on a harvest sheet for the day before delivery. Sod is normally harvested to order the day before it is delivered to allow time for the harvest, loading of the trucks, and actual delivery.

The harvest supervisor uses the harvest sheet to fill the customer orders. A pallet tag listing the type of grass, square footage, number of pallets, and order number is attached to each pallet of harvested sod. To help avoid confusion, Eucre Sod's Elite tall fescue pallet tags are printed on gold paper and the Santa Ana hybrid bermudagrass tags are on green paper. Distribution personnel then load the sod onto the trucks according to destination. When the sod has been delivered, the order taker prepares and mails the invoice. The entire process, from taking the order through to harvest, delivery, and billing, is coordinated in the Eucre Sod front office.

Credit processing

Most of the U.S. economy operates on credit, and the sod industry is no exception. This is one of many functions in the firm that must be carefully monitored.

Open accounts at Eucre Sod are approved by the general manager, since the company does not have a full-time credit manager. Normal terms for customers with good credit specify a 2 percent discount if the invoice is paid within 10 days. The bill is due and payable 30 days from the date of delivery. The manager must act to collect accounts that exceed the 30-day limit.

Customers without open accounts or with delinquent credit balances must buy sod on a cash-on-delivery (COD) basis. The delivery personnel receive payment before the sod is left on the site. When COD orders are to be delivered, but the customers either are not present to pay or cannot pay, the sod is returned to the farm. The sales and order staff try to sell it before it gets back, at a discount if necessary. If it is not sold that day, it is dumped and taken as a loss. On occasion there might be a little-league field or church where a donation can be arranged.

Perhaps the most traumatic task for the Eucre Sod administration is managing credit. It starts when the sales staff convinces a new customer to buy from Eucre Sod and that customer wants credit. The decision as to whether to allow an open account and establish a credit limit is nearly always based upon very little information, often of questionable reliability. The customer has usually given three or four references of suppliers that have been pretty well kept current. However, there may be several other suppliers with whom the customer's accounts are delinquent. The standard credit rating firms are often of little use because of the size and nature of sod customers. If the credit policy is too restrictive, sales suffer; if too loose, bad debt losses increase.

The difficult part of credit management is the calling of delinquent accounts. Sod company general managers may be ill equipped to withstand the dramatic creativity of customers with overdue accounts. Though one of the vital functions of a business, credit management historically is handled poorly by small to mid-sized sod companies.

Planning and budgeting

Planning is important for every business, particularly if there is external interest in the company. Partners or stockholders may or may not wish to know that the management has a "business plan," but major lenders often require it.

A business plan can be fairly simple. The plan should include a description of what the business is, who the principals are and what their backgrounds are (lenders nearly always want to see personal financial statements), what the market is like, and why the borrowers expect the whole enterprise to succeed.

As a part of the business plan, investors and lenders will also want to see a sales forecast, a capital budget, an expense budget, a pro forma balance sheet, asset requirements, and loan requirements. Lenders will want to become confident in the sod company's ability to repay a loan.

Business plan

Eucre Sod produces turfgrass sod on 120 acres of land 22 miles south of Watertown, and has a 5-year option on 150 adjacent acres. The company markets and delivers its own product.

Eucre Sod's product is lawn-type grasses grown to the point that they can be severed just below the soil level, physically picked up, carried to another site, laid on that site, and made to grow into a lawn. It is a perishable product and should be installed within 36 hours from the time of harvest. After installation, the new lawn knits in a few days into a high-quality turfgrass sward.

Eucre Sod is organized as a partnership with equal ownership between the principals. Mr. Allen has extensive experience in agriculture, having grown up on a farm and worked for a major farming company in the southwest. Ms. Baker has served as regional sales manager for a national manufacturing company for 15 years. Dr. Chew is a successful neurosurgeon with a highly developed interest in gardening.

The primary market is new home lawns in Watertown, its suburbs, and the surrounding county. The company sells a significant amount of sod for commercial and institutional lawns, golf courses, and parks. Eucre Sod sells only wholesale to landscape contractors, nurseries, garden centers, and other professional users including golf course superintendents and government agencies.

Last year there were 9,000 single family housing starts in the county, according to the publication of construction reports. The average front lawn is 1,000 square feet and the average back lawn is 1,200 square feet. The potential for new home lawn sales last year was 455 acres. Commercial and institutional purchasers represented another 100 acres of potential sod sales.

Two sod companies compete with Eucre Sod. Together the two sold about 120 acres to go with Eucre Sod's 80 acres of sales last year. Thirty-six percent of the potential sod market in the area was tapped. Eucre Sod can still expand sales to 100 acres and fill an immediate need in the market.

The National Bank estimates that, if the economy holds, new single family dwelling construction in the county will increase at 5 percent per year for the next 5 years. It also estimates that the commercial and institutional sod potential will increase at about the same rate. This will put the potential sod market at slightly over 700 acres in 5 years.

Budget

The sod producer's budget is important to lenders, investors, and management. It is a valuable management tool. Obviously, no one can forecast with any certainty what will happen to a business over the next year, but sod company managers must put the effort and thought into what they think will take place or what they expect the companies to do.

In commerce, budgets are guidelines and only guidelines. Unfortunately, in large companies, budgets are often treated as if they were written in stone. In Eucre Sod, the management has an appreciation of the value of the budget as a tool.

The Eucre Sod budget begins with a sales forecast (table 1). There are various means of arriving at predicted sales figures, and one is to correlate sod sales mathematically to some reported economic factor such as local area housing starts or building permits. This method is relatively accurate in the short term, but does require a historical record of sales.

The "gut" feeling should not be overlooked. If the sod company manager or sales staff have a good feel for the market, their estimates should not be taken lightly. As a part of this, the manager should be aware of the economic forecasts for the area that are made routinely by local and regional banks.

Market surveys can also be helpful, but they are only as good as the samples and techniques of the surveyors. Interpreting market surveys can be risky.

The next step in building the Eucre Sod budget is to determine whether and how production can meet the Elite tall fescue sales and Santa Ana bermudagrass sales forecasts (tables 2 and 3). The month-by-month sales forecast is run across the bottom of a chart. Time periods shorter than a month are more trouble than they are worth and, thus, less likely to be used. Longer periods, such as quarters, are meaningless as working tools. Individual fields are listed and the available acres shown. Available acres are those expected to be available for sales, with anticipated losses taken into account.

Projected monthly sales are subtracted from the sod availability, and the month-end inventory balance is shown at the bottom of table 2 and

Table 1. Eucre Sod sales forecast 19XY (next year)*

	Jan.	Feb.	Mar.	Apr.	May	June	July	Aug.	Sept.	Oct.	Nov.	Dec.	Total
Acres	4.0	4.0	6.0	11.0	14.5	18.0	13.5	11.5	9.0	8.0	5.5	5.0	110.0
Dollars ($\times$1,000)	33.2	33.2	49.8	91.3	120.4	149.4	112.1	95.5	74.7	66.4	45.7	41.5	913.0

*Average expected selling price $8,300/acre ($0.19/sq. ft.), and sales include 100 acres of Elite and 10 acres of Santa Ana.

Table 2. Eucre Sod Elite tall fescue inventory forecast 19XY (next year)

Field	Available acres*	Mature, unharvested acres												
		Jan.	Feb.	Mar.	Apr.	May	June	July	Aug.	Sept.	Oct.	Nov.	Dec.	Total
A	20.0	12.0	8.0	4.0	N†	→	→	→	20.0	17.5	9.5	2.5	P‡	
B	20.0	P	→	→	→	→	→	→	→	20.0	20.0	20.0	17.0	
C	10.0	→	→	10.0	10.0	8.5	P	→	→	→	→	→	→	
D	20.0	→	→	→	20.0	20.0	15.5	P	→	→	→	→	→	
E	20.0		N	→	→	→	20.0	19.5	7.5	P	→	→	→	
F	10.0	10.0	10.0	10.0	8.5	P	→	→	→	→	→	→	→	
Acres sold		4.0	4.0	5.5	10.0	13.0	16.0	12.0	10.0	8.0	7.0	5.5	5.0	100.0
Balance		18.0	14.0	18.5	28.5	15.5	19.5	7.5	17.5	29.5	22.5	17.0	12.0	

*Number of acres available for sale after deducting 15% for losses.
†N = Planted with netting
‡P = Planted without netting

Table 3. Eucre Sod Santa Ana bermudagrass inventory forecast 19XY (next year)

Field	Available acres*	Mature, unharvested acres												
		Jan.	Feb.	Mar.	Apr.	May	June	July	Aug.	Sept.	Oct.	Nov.	Dec.	Total
G	10.0	10.0	10.0	10.0	9.5	8.5	7.0	5.0	3.5	2.0	1.0	.0	.0	
Regrowth								.5	1.5	3.5	5.0	6.5	6.5	
Acres sold		.0	.0	.5	1.0	1.5	2.0	1.5	1.5	1.0	1.0	.0	.0	10.0
Balance		10.0	10.0	9.5	8.5	7.0	5.0	4.0	3.5	4.5	5.0	6.5	6.5	

*Number of acres available for sale after deducting 15% for losses.
Bermudagrass is allowed to regrow and not replanted.

table 3. If an Elite tall fescue product shortage appears in a given month, the manager can change the planting technique (e.g., use plastic netting) or take other steps to cover the expected shortage. Even the growth rate of Santa Ana bermudagrass can sometimes be accelerated to cover a hole in production.

Using table 4, Eucre Sod management estimates when each Elite tall fescue field will be ready for harvest. A table such as this can be made for each sod farm location, if growing conditions vary, and for each type of turfgrass. The table lends a consistency to the estimating decisions. It is also useful later on for determining inventory valuation. A similar table can be constructed for the Santa Ana. Since the Santa Ana production is so small, Eucre Sod management has not made a chart for it. The inventory maturity is estimated by merely looking at the field.

Next, Eucre Sod management sets up a labor budget (table 5). It is a truism in business that dollars follow people. The first step in labor budgeting is to project the number of people needed in each job. Then,

Table 4. Eucre Sod Elite tall fescue inventory maturity forecast chart*

Jan.	Feb.	Mar.	Apr.	May	June	July	Aug.	Sept.	Oct.	Nov.	Dec.
0	10	20	30	50	70	80	90	100			
	0	10	25	45	65	75	85	100			
		0	10	30	50	60	70	85	100		
			0	20	40	50	60	75	90	100	
				0	20	30	40	55	70	85	100
100					0	10	20	35	60	75	90
70	80	90	100			0	10	25	40	55	60
65	75	85	95	100			0	10	25	40	55
55	65	75	85	100				0	15	30	45
40	50	60	70	85	100				0	15	30
25	35	45	55	70	85	95	100			0	15
10	20	30	40	55	70	80	90	100			0

If planted with plastic netting:

Jan.	Feb.	Mar.	Apr.	May	June	July	Aug.	Sept.	Oct.	Nov.	Dec.
0	10	20	50	80	100						
	0	10	40	70	100						
		0	20	50	80	100					
			0	30	60	80	100				
				0	30	50	70	90	100		
					0	20	40	60	90	100	
						0	20	40	70	100	
100							0	20	50	80	95
85	95	100						0	30	60	75
55	65	75	95	100				0	30		45
25	35	45	75	95	100				0		15
10	20	30	60	90	100						0

*Months with "0" are planting dates; months with "100" are harvest ready.

The numbers in the intervening months indicate the percent maturity in each month of growth. For example: sod planted in March (0) would be mature in October (100). It would be 30% mature in May, 60% in July, etc.

step by step, determine the amount of money that will be needed. Labor costs can very easily get out of control and directly impact profits. Considerable thought should be given to the labor budget. The supplies budget and water budget can be set by a similar technique.

The general budget draws from as much specific information as is available, as well as some estimating. Table 6 shows the Eucre Sod budget by line item according to the chart of accounts. Comparisons to the monthly accounting report of expenditures are easily made as the year progresses. In budgeting, it is not necessary to estimate down to the penny. Keeping in mind that the budget is a guideline, Eucre Sod uses decimal values in thousands of dollars. These numbers are much easier to work with than the large values they represent.

Balance sheet

A balance sheet is a report of the condition of a business at a certain point in time. It is sometimes thought of as a photograph of one day's business. Accounts receivable and accounts payable change daily, and so therefore does the balance sheet.

One side of the Eucre Sod balance sheet (table 7) shows the business assets. Current assets are items that are liquid—they can be turned into cash almost immediately. That is in theory only, since in reality accounts receivable (money owed by customers) can be difficult to collect. Fixed assets also represent cash, but are not so liquid. Land, equipment, and the like are fixed assets. In many cases a long-term lease on land is considered both as asset and as liability. Land and other tangible assets are always listed by their purchase price, not by current market value. The purchase price is a hard number, while the current market value is an estimate and not considered reliable by accounting standards. For this reason, assets are often undervalued if land has appreciated. Equipment is listed as to its purchase price after deducting depreciation.

The other side of the balance sheet is for liabilities, the debt the firm owes. Current liabilities are those debts due and payable within 1 year. This includes accounts payable (money owed to suppliers), lease payments, and mortgage payments. Long-term liabilities are debts that must be paid in more than 1 year. For example, after deducting 1 year's payment as a current liability, the mortgage is a long-term debt.

The liability side of the balance sheet also shows equity. Equity is equal to the assets minus the liabilities. This is determined by subtracting total liabilities from total assets, and is used to balance the liability side to the asset side—hence the name *balance sheet*. Equity has more uses than just balancing the balance sheet; it shows how much the owners have invested in the business or what the value of the business is to the owners after all debts are paid.

One of the first tests that lenders will make on the business is to divide the total liabilities by the equity to get the debt-to-equity ratio. If

Table 5. Eucre Sod production labor requirements for 19XY (next year)

Description	Jan.	Feb.	Mar.	Apr.	May
Weeks/month	4	4	5	4	4
Irrigation					
People	2	2	2	2	2
Hours/week/person	35	35	40	44	44
Hours/month/person	140	140	200	176	176
Dollars/hour	6.25	6.25	6.25	6.25	6.25
Dollars/person	875.00	875.00	1,250.00	1,100.00	1,100.00
Irrigation dollars	1,750.00	1,750.00	2,500.00	2,200.00	2,200.00
Fieldwork & harvest					
People	2	2	3	3	4
Hours/week/person	35	35	40	44	44
Hours/month/person	140	140	200	176	176
Dollars/hour	6.00	6.00	6.00	6.00	6.00
Dollars/person	840.00	840.00	1,200.00	1,056.00	1,056.00
Field work & harvest dollars	1,680.00	1,680.00	3,600.00	3,168.00	4,224.00
Field supervisor					
People	1	1	1	1	1
Salary	1,800.00	1,800.00	1,800.00	1,800.00	1,800.00
Total production					
labor dollars	5,230.00	5,230.00	7,900.00	7,168.00	8,224.00

there is too much debt for the equity, then the company is overextended and a bad loan risk. If there is too much equity, the management is not making effective use of its assets. Eucre Sod has a debt-to-equity ratio of 2:1, which would usually be considered acceptable in an agricultural enterprise.

Eucre Sod shows a current asset value for inventory. Using table 4, the percentage of Elite inventory maturity is determined and the percentage of Santa Ana inventory maturity is estimated and both are recorded in table 8, where the dollar value of the total inventory is calculated. For inventory purposes, each field is physically measured at planting and again when some change occurs (e.g., damage from a flood). At the end of each month, the fields being harvested are measured to calculate how much sod is left. Losses are determined by subtracting the number of acres in the field at planting from the number of acres sold out of the field.

When measuring the fields, some method must be used to assign a value to immature turf. In many industries, this would be called work-in-process. Eucre Sod uses table 4 to put a percentage mature value on

	June	July	Aug.	Sept.	Oct.	Nov.	Dec.	Total
	5	4	4	5	4	4	5	
	2	2	2	2	2	2	2	
	50	50	50	50	44	40	35	
	250	200	200	250	176	160	175	
	6.25	6.25	6.25	6.25	6.25	6.25	6.25	
	1,562.50	1,250.00	1,250.00	1,562.50	1,100.00	1,000.00	1,093.75	14,018.75
	3,125.00	2,500.00	2,500.00	3,125.00	2,200.00	2,000.00	2,187.50	28,037.50
	4	3	3	3	3	3	2	
	44	44	44	40	40	40	35	
	220	176	176	200	160	160	175	
	6.00	6.00	6.00	6.00	6.00	6.00	6.00	
	1,320.00	1,056.00	1,056.00	1,200.00	960.00	960.00	1,050.00	12,594.00
	5,280.00	3,168.00	3,168.00	3,600.00	2,880.00	2,880.00	2,100.00	37,428.00
	1	1	1	1	1	1	1	
	1,800.00	1,800.00	1,800.00	1,800.00	1,800.00	1,800.00	1,800.00	21,600.00
	10,205.00	7,468.00	7,468.00	8,525.00	6,880.00	6,680.00	6,087.50	87,065.50

each immature Elite field, and multiplies it by the planted acreage. The product is then multiplied by the average direct cost per acre, which is determined from the financial statement. Production costs are considered to be the direct costs.

Inventory bases the value on the actual dollars invested and not on the projected market value. Other costs, such as distribution, sales expenses, and administration, are not considered as input into the production fields.

Financial statement

The financial statement (table 9) is of great value to Eucre Sod's manager. This statement lists the dollars spent by the firm and reported by the accountants. By comparing the financial statement to the budget, the manager can tell how the business is doing from month to month.

Gross profit essentially shows the Eucre Sod management that variable costs are being covered. *Net operating income,* in this case, is the profit before taxes. In most year-end financial statements, taxes get a thorough treatment.

Table 6. Eucre Sod general budget 19XY (next year)

	Jan.	Feb.	Mar.
Elite acres sold	4.0	4.0	5.5
Santa Ana acres sold	.0	.0	.5
Sales income (× $1,000)	33.2	33.2	49.8
Production costs (× $1,000)			
Direct labor	5.2	5.2	7.9
Payroll taxes	.5	.5	.8
Contract labor			
Insurance	9.0		
Direct supplies	.5	5.0	.5
Other supplies	.2	.2	.3
Water	2.0	2.0	3.5
Fuel/vehicle	.5	.5	1.5
Equipment rent			
Equipment repair	.5	1.0	1.0
Depreciation	3.8	3.8	3.8
Amortized fumigation	1.6	1.6	1.6
Miscellaneous	.1	.1	.1
Total production costs	23.9	19.9	21.0
Distribution costs (× $1,000)			
Labor	1.8	1.8	2.5
Payroll taxes	.3	.3	.3
Supplies	1.8	1.8	2.5
Fuel/vehicle	1.4	1.4	1.9
Equipment rent			
Equipment repair	.2	.5	.5
Depreciation	1.6	1.6	1.6
Miscellaneous	.1	.1	.1
Total distribution costs	7.2	7.5	9.4
Sales expenses (× $1,000)			
Salaries	3.8	3.8	3.8
Payroll taxes	.4	.4	.4
Auto/travel	.5	.5	.8
Equipment repair	.1		
Supplies	.1	.1	.1
Advertising	.5	.5	.8
Miscellaneous	.1	.1	.1
Total sales expenses	5.5	5.4	6.0
General and administrative expenses (× $1,000)			
Salaries	7.0	7.0	7.0
Payroll taxes	.7	.7	.7
Insurance	6.0		
Taxes/licenses	.2	.2	.2
Equipment rent		.1	
Interest	.4	.4	.4
Land rent	3.0	3.0	3.0
Telephone/utilities	.8	.8	.8
Legal/accounting	.8	.8	.8
Office expenses	.1	.1	.1
Auto/travel	.2	.2	.2
Miscellaneous	.1	.1	.1
Total general & administrative expenses	19.3	13.4	13.3
Total costs and expenses	55.9	46.2	49.7
Sales minus costs (loss)	(22.7)	(13.0)	.1

Apr.	May	June	July	Aug.	Sept.	Oct.	Nov.	Dec.	Total
10.0	13.0	16.0	12.0	10.0	8.0	7.0	5.5	5.0	100.0
1.0	1.5	2.0	1.5	1.5	1.0	1.0	.0	.0	10.0
91.3	120.4	149.4	112.1	95.5	74.7	66.4	45.7	41.5	913.2
7.2	8.2	10.2	8.5	8.5	8.5	5.9	5.7	6.1	87.1
.7	.8	1.0	.9	.9	.9	.6	.6	.6	8.8
2.0	2.0								4.0
		9.0							18.0
.5	5.0	.5	.5	.5	.5	5.0	.5	.5	19.5
.5	.5	.4	.4	.4	.4	.8	.4	.2	4.7
6.0	7.0	10.0	17.0	17.0	15.0	9.0	7.0	1.0	96.5
3.0	2.0	2.0	1.5	1.5	2.0	1.0	.8	.5	16.8
.5	.5								1.0
.5	.5	.5	.5	.5	.5	.5	.5	.2	6.7
3.8	3.8	3.8	3.8	3.8	3.8	3.8	3.8	3.8	45.6
1.6	1.6	1.6	1.6	1.6	1.6	1.6	1.6	1.6	19.2
.1	.1	.1	.1	.1	.1	.1	.1	.1	1.2
26.4	32.0	39.1	34.8	34.8	33.3	28.3	21.0	14.6	329.1
4.6	6.0	7.4	5.5	4.6	3.7	3.2	2.5	2.3	46.0
.4	.5	.6	.6	.5	.4	.3	.3	.3	4.8
4.5	5.9	7.2	5.4	4.5	3.6	3.2	2.5	2.3	45.0
3.4	4.4	5.4	4.1	3.4	2.7	2.4	1.9	1.7	34.0
.5	.5	.5	.5	.5					2.5
1.0	1.5	1.5	1.0	1.0	1.0	.5	.5	2.0	11.2
1.6	1.6	1.6	1.6	1.6	1.6	1.6	1.6	1.6	19.2
.1	.1	.1	.1	.1	.1	.1	.1	.1	1.2
16.1	20.5	24.3	18.8	16.2	13.1	11.3	9.4	10.3	163.9
3.8	3.8	3.8	3.8	3.8	3.8	3.8	3.8	3.8	45.6
.4	.4	.4	.4	.4	.4	.4	.4	.4	4.6
1.0	1.5	1.5	1.5	1.5	.8	.8	.5	.5	11.4
			.1	.1	.1			.1	.5
.1	.1	.1	.1	.1	.1	.1	.1	.1	1.2
.8	.8	.8	.5	.2	.2	.2	.2	.2	5.7
.1	.1	.1	.1	.1	.1	.1	.1	.1	1.2
6.2	6.7	6.8	6.5	6.2	5.4	5.4	5.1	5.2	70.2
7.0	7.0	7.0	7.0	7.0	7.0	7.0	7.0	7.0	84.0
.7	.7	.7	.7	.7	.7	.7	.7	.7	8.4
		6.0							12.0
.2	.2	.2	.2	.2	.2	.2	.2	.2	2.4
.1		.1		.1		.1		.1	.6
.4	.4	.4	.4	.4	.4	.4	.4	.4	4.8
3.0	3.0	3.0	3.0	3.0	3.0	3.0	3.0	3.0	36.0
.8	.8	.8	.8	.8	.8	.8	.8	.8	9.6
.8	.8	.8	.8	.8	.8	.8	.8	.8	9.6
.1	.1	.1	.1	.1	.1	.1	.1	.1	1.2
.2	.2	.2	.2	.2	.2	.2	.2	.2	2.4
.1	.1	.1	.1	.1	.1	.1	.1	.1	1.2
13.4	13.3	19.4	13.3	13.4	13.3	13.4	13.3	13.4	172.2
62.1	72.5	89.6	73.4	70.6	65.1	58.3	48.8	43.4	735.4
29.2	48.0	59.8	38.7	24.9	9.6	8.1	(3.1)	(1.9)	177.8

Table 7. Eucre Sod balance sheet: December 31, 19XX (past year)

Assets			
Current			
Cash	$15,375.18		
Accounts receivable	$45,450.37		
Inventory	$237,705.00		
Total current assets		$298,530.55	
Fixed			
Lease (land)	$180,000.00		
Equipment	$724,935.20		
Other assets	$85,000.00		
Total fixed assets		$989,935.20	
Total assets			$1,288,465.75
Liabilities			
Current			
Accounts payable	$34,748.39		
Short-term debt	$339,652.32		
Total current liabilities		$374,400.71	
Long term			
Long-term debt		$469,236.22	
Total liabilities		$843,636.93	
Equity		$444,828.82	
Total liabilities and equity			$1,288,465.75

Table 8. Eucre Sod inventory: December 31, 19XX (past year)

Field	Total acres	Percentage mature*	Equivalent mature acres[†]	Inventory value[‡]
A	24	100	24.0	$82,800
B	24	0	.0	0
C	12	80	9.6	33,120
D	24	70	16.8	57,960
E	24	0	.0	0
F	12	100	12.0	41,400
G[§]	12	100	6.5	22,425
Total	132			$237,705

*Percent maturity of the sod in the field.
[†]Percent maturity times production acres.
[‡]Direct production costs per acre ($3,450) times equivalent mature acres.
[§]Santa Ana is constantly regrowing and difficult to evaluate. Always use either 0 or 100 percent maturity at year end.

Table 9. Eucre Sod financial statement: Year ending December 31, 19XX (past year)

Sales income	$664,000.00		
Production costs		Sales expenses	
Direct labor	69,680.00	Salaries	36,480.00
Payroll taxes	7,040.00	Payroll taxes	3,648.00
Contract labor	3,200.00	Auto/travel	9,120.00
Insurance	18,000.00	Equipment repair	400.00
Direct supplies	15,600.00	Supplies	960.00
Other supplies	3,776.00	Advertising	4,560.00
Water	77,200.00	Miscellaneous	960.00
Fuel/vehicle	13,440.00	Total sales expenses	$56,128.00
Equipment rent	800.00		
Equipment repair	5,360.00	General & administrative expenses	
Depreciation	45,600.00	Salaries	67,200.00
Amortized fumigation	15,360.00	Payroll taxes	6,720.00
Miscellaneous	960.00	Insurance	12,000.00
Total production costs	$276,016.00	Taxes/licenses	2,400.00
		Equipment rent	480.00
Distribution costs		Interest	3,840.00
Labor	36,800.00	Land rent	28,800.00
Payroll taxes	3,840.00	Telephone/utilities	7,680.00
Supplies	36,000.00	Legal/accounting	9,600.00
Fuel/vehicle	27,200.00	Office expenses	960.00
Equipment rent	2,000.00	Auto/travel	1,920.00
Equipment repair	8,960.00	Miscellaneous	960.00
Depreciation	19,200.00	Total general & administrative	
Miscellaneous	960.00	expenses	$142,560.00
Total distribution costs	$134,960.00		
		Total expenses	$198,688.00
Total costs of sales	$410,976.00		
Gross profit (loss)	$253,024.00	Net operating income (loss)	$54,336.00

3

Sales

Eucre Sod

Eucre Sod produces two sod products for the Watertown area market—Elite tall fescue blend and Santa Ana hybrid bermudagrass. Elite is a blend of three tall fescues that are excellent performers in the Watertown area. Santa Ana hybrid bermudagrass is a durable, well-adapted turfgrass for high-traffic areas as well as home lawns. The two products provide the market with turf that can be used in many situations. Besides providing superior sod products and high-quality turf, Eucre Sod is a service-oriented company. Customers stay loyal due to service both before and after the sale.

The consumer is not really interested in whether a lawn is installed as sod, seed, or stolons; the product being purchased is a growing lawn. How soon the consumer wants the lawn is the sod grower's concern.

Eucre Sod has identified the following market segments in Watertown, along with the amount of traffic a lawn will get in each market segment:

1. Homeowners without children (no traffic)

2. Homeowners with children (moderate traffic)

3. Commercial lawn owners (no traffic)

4. Government agencies—ornamental lawns (no traffic)

5. Government agencies—recreational lawns (high traffic)

6. Sports fields (high traffic)

7. Golf courses (moderate traffic)

All of the market segments are interested in aesthetics, but their requirements for traffic vary. Some segments want a specific playing quality, others durability, and others are more concerned with low maintenance.

Eucre Sod has decided to focus on segments 1 and 2, while still making lesser sales efforts to the other segments. The company's sod products fit the requirements of these two segments nicely and they represent a sizable sales potential. Eucre Sod will "pull" the products through the market channels by using promotion, and will place advertising in the Watertown newspaper's garden section, business/real estate section, and sports section. The timing of the advertisements is being scheduled. In addition, Eucre Sod will participate in cooperative advertising with several retail nurseries and landscape firms.

Developers of single-family home tracts generally landscape only model homes unless sales are slow. Through an agreement with a licensed landscape contractor, Eucre Sod plans to offer an installed lawn package that the developer can make available to home buyers at the time of the new home sale. The new homeowner can move in with a sodded lawn in place and the developer can average about $300 in additional profit per home, with no input other than sales and collecting the money. Eucre Sod will provide promotional materials, install the sod, and service any complaints.

Steve Zapatas, the Eucre Sod salesperson, will continue to make calls throughout the traditional market channels—retail nurseries and residential landscapers—but will also spend a great deal of time working with housing developers. If he can get consumers to request Eucre Sod products, sales efforts will be more productive.

In most sod markets, the competitors sell essentially the same products. Plant breeders are providing very good cultivars and most are available to all growers. Proprietary cultivars may have advantages if they are superior in one or two minor characteristics. For the most part, though, each sod company must create a way to distinguish its product from those of its competitors.

After delivery to the customer, the new sod is installed in the landscape.

Product differentiation

The two simplest means of product differentiation, and the most difficult to sustain, are quality and service. *Quality* is the uniform appearance and density of the turfgrass—fresh, cleanly cut, and neatly stacked sod pads—and good sod strength. *Service* involves prompt, timely deliveries, neatly stacked pallets, immediate attention to complaints, accurate orders, and friendly, competent staff.

Management must be committed to quality and service. That commitment must be the daily operating policy of all employees. Once that policy, attitude, and commitment are in place, a companywide orientation toward the customer develops. A reputation for looking out for the customer can even outweigh a price difference.

Product differentiation can also be accomplished by using a brand name. Most sod is purchased by a customer who calls the company and places an order, rather than by a company sales representative who makes a call and writes it up. Brand names are easily remembered, especially if the customer has had a good experience with the product. Where sod is sold through retail outlets, a branded product connotes quality to the retail customer. The virtues of a sod product are easy to tie to a brand name in advertising and sales calls.

Seeded grasses are usually planted in *blends* of cultivars or in *mixtures* of cultivars or species. By creating a brand name for the product, the sod grower is not violating an existing trademark of the grass breeder. Advertising can be used to shout the benefits of having "the best of several worlds" in the blend, because of the several grasses present.

In a small or developing market, the grower will probably try a shotgun approach to selling. In a larger market with several competitors, a new or established grower may want to identify specific customer groups upon which to concentrate sales efforts.

Market segmentation

Market segmentation is simply the division of a market into groups. Landscape contractors, retail nurseries, and institutions are three wholesale market segments. Direct retail sales is a segment that can be split into do-it-yourself, custom-installed, or grower-installed groups. Geographic areas are also possible market segments. There are many possible market segments, and at some point the sod producer must decide which ones will return the most sales for the money.

Small sod producers can often identify a niche in the market that the larger companies have overlooked or cannot afford to spend time on. By exploiting a niche the grower can avoid head-to-head competition with the large firms.

The sod producer may be able to serve an out-of-the-way area inconvenient to others. Some landscape contractors like to pick up relatively small quantities of sod on the same day they place the order. A small grower can cater to this business and build on it. Direct retail sales, custom installation, sports fields, and model homes all are potential niches for a new or small grower.

Distribution channels

A channel of distribution in the market is the means by which a product gets to the consumer. The most common distribution channel for sod goes from the grower, through a landscape contractor or sod installer, and to the consumer. Another frequently used channel goes through a nursery to the consumer. In both cases, the sod product is normally "pushed" through the channel—the sod is ordered by the installer or the nursery, which has already sold it to the consumer.

Growers large and small have successfully sold by direct retail. There are examples of everything from classy retail lawn supply stores to "cut your own sod" operations. With the latter, customers seldom actually cut the sod, but they do roll it and load it. Another successful marketing tool is installation by the sod company. This is done either by having a full-time installation crew or by subcontracting a crew. The sod customer buys the sod installed and the sod company coordinates the delivery and installation.

It is more expensive for the grower to "pull" the product through the market distribution channel than to "push" it. Pulling the product requires that the consumer first be sold, and then request that an intermediary provide the specific sod. This is accomplished with extensive advertising in mass media or in targeted publications such as garden magazines to develop sod product recognition.

Promotion

Advertising and promotion are often used to build a positive image or product recognition. Even though this approach is most effective when focused upon a specific market segment, a more general approach has its place in the marketing program.

The most common type of unfocused advertising for sod companies is the telephone book's yellow pages. Many growers feel that the return is poor on a yellow pages advertisement, but few growers are willing to miss having one. In particular, sod growers who sell by direct retail, pulling the product through the channel, put a high value on telephone book advertising.

Landscape trade journals can be important media for advertising turfgrass sod, especially for large companies selling wholesale. These publications may not be particularly useful for the small grower since the circulation usually covers a very large geographic area and the advertisements can be expensive.

Local newspapers and advertising circulars are used extensively in retail sales. Growers who sell only wholesale also make extensive use of these media via cooperative advertising with retail outlets such as nurseries and garden centers. The sod grower normally pays for a percentage of the retailer's advertisement and provides a logo and some copy. Payment to the dealer may take the form of credit on future sales.

Radio and television advertising is expensive, but some sod companies do use these media. The electronic media can be used to establish a strong product identity. Consumers will ask for XYZ grass if they heard about it on the radio or saw it on television. Again, this expensive technique pulls the product through the marketing channel.

Trade shows provide an effective means for getting the word out to customers, but are very expensive. The grower pays for booth space, has a display built, and pays the wages of personnel who staff the booth, often for several days. The big advantage of a trade show is that nearly all the visitors to the show are potential customers. A well-designed display can easily pay for itself in increased sales if the show is well attended.

Membership in trade organizations such as a landscape contractors association can be useful. By attending the meetings, a grower can develop a rapport with the more active members of the industry. Trade organizations give the grower an opportunity to give something back to the industry and are good for image building.

The volume discount is another form of promotion that is almost required, because everyone offers it in nearly all sod markets. Some growers only offer discounts on a single sale and others record the accumulated volume from an individual customer over a period of time, and give progressive discounts. The latter method requires additional bookkeeping, but it can build customer loyalty.

Sales staff

The most effective means of selling turfgrass sod is still through a hard-working salesperson. All of the other marketing techniques usually act as support. A salesperson can move the product.

Eucre Sod pays its sales staff a salary plus a commission. Mr. Zapatas receives $1,725 per month salary ($20,700 per year) and a 3 percent commission. Since he is the only salesperson on the staff, he receives the commission on all sales. If the budgeted sales of $830,000 are met, Mr.

Zapatas will earn $45,600 for the year. Any reduced prices that are negotiated and any bad debts will cut into Mr. Zapata's income. The budget (table 6) shows a monthly sales salary of $3,800. This figure assumes that the sales projection will be realized in equal portions over the 12 months to make budget preparation easier. Showing the salary and commission on separate lines would be a reasonable alternative.

Sales staff can be compensated in any of a number of ways; *salary, salary plus commission, draw plus commission, salary plus bonus,* and *straight commission* are the most common. *Salary* is a monthly wage that does not depend upon the hours worked or the amount sold. Some salespersons are very effective with this, because they are comfortable knowing how much money they are going to make.

Salary plus commission provides a living wage, but not a comfortable one, and adds the incentive of being able to increase earnings by increasing sales. Knowing the salary is there to fall back on if sales are bad in a given period yet having the ability to greatly increase a month's income can be a good motivator for some individuals.

A *draw* is an amount of money the company loans to the salesperson, who repays it out of commission. A draw provides some wage in the event of a bad sales month, and it too can be a good motivator if the commission is high enough.

Salary plus bonus provides a good wage to the salesperson and allows for additional money if certain goals are met. The goals can be monthly, quarterly, or annual. If the goals are achievable and the bonus is sufficient, this method can be a good motivator.

Straight commission is very difficult for some salespersons to deal with, yet others prefer it. No salary or advance is provided. The salesperson earns a percentage of everything he or she sells. It can take a long time before a salesperson can earn a living wage under this method. He or she must build a clientele and establish a large number of contacts. Straight commission is rare in the sod industry.

The compensation methods involving incentives require that the firm maintain accurate bookkeeping and track all orders. If there are two or more salespersons, the grower must decide how to assign credit for a sale. Some growers credit the sale according to the location of the customer's office. With this method, it is possible for a salesperson to make a sale to a customer located in his or her territory, but if the sod is delivered in another person's territory, another salesperson not credited with the sale must service the site. This is often unsatisfactory.

Another method of crediting the sale is by the delivery location. This is the reverse of the previous situation and may penalize the salesperson who did the work to get the sale.

One consistent problem with all the incentive compensation methods is the amount earned by the salesperson. It is not unusual to have a compensation or commission package in which management believes that the salesperson earns too much money. Some companies have even cut their incentives in the middle of a sales period. Understandably, when that happens morale collapses.

An incentive must be calculated very carefully. If the company decides that it can afford to pay a given percentage to an individual in exchange for increased sales and that individual accepts those terms, then payment should be made no matter how much is sold. A company can do great harm to its profits by tinkering with incentive programs. A commission agreement is considered a contract whether signed or not, and the employer could legally be held to the terms of the agreement. The renegotiation can take place for the next year, if either party is dissatisfied. Bonuses should be based upon attainable goals, and should be negotiated with input from the management and sales staff.

4

Soil Preparation and Planting

Eucre Sod

The Eucre Sod management chose the site for the sod farm by considering five criteria: distance from the market, accessibility, water availability and quality, soil type, and wind, in that order. Eucre Sod is located only 22 miles from Watertown, an easy haul. The farm is on a paved road 2 miles from a major highway. Water is readily available and the quality is good. The soil is a sandy loam with neutral pH, low salinity, and no stones or rocks. The farm is not in a particularly windblown area, and the irrigation system will not be seriously affected by the consistent afternoon breezes.

Eucre Sod grows two sod products: a blend of three tall fescues and a hybrid bermudagrass. The blend is called Elite. Production chose the three grasses in the blend from the results of tests conducted at the University of California. A local seed distributor purchases sod-quality seed and custom mixes it for Eucre Sod.

Santa Ana hybrid bermudagrass was developed at the University of California, Riverside, and is very well adapted to the Watertown area. The original Santa Ana stolons were purchased from a sod grower in another part of the state to plant ½ acre. Eucre Sod has harvested and planted its own stolons, expanding to the current 10 acres of bermudagrass.

The Elite tall fescue fields are plowed, disked, cultipacked, and landplaned before seeding. Production has begun rotary tilling behind harvest in an attempt to reduce land preparation time. This has worked so far, but every 2 years each field will be plowed, disked, cultipacked, and landplaned.

Every 5 years, each field is fumigated with methyl bromide. This eliminates nearly all weeds and nematodes, plus many turf diseases. The broadleaf weeds that escape fumigation are relatively easy to control with selective weed killers. Insects and diseases usually cause no problems for several months after fumigation.

The sod fields are seeded at 350 pounds per acre of Elite seed. A drop seeder with ring rollers plants one-half of the seed in parallel passes, and then the other half in parallel passes perpendicular to and over the top of the first planting. The two plantings seem to increase stand uniformity. After seeding, the netting is applied perpendicular to the irrigation system. Each time the net-layer makes a pass across the field, aluminum pipe is laid on the netting. If the pipe keeps pace with the net-layer, there is no problem keeping the netting on the ground.

Production's goal is to be able to turn the water on the newly seeded field 2 weeks after the last sod is harvested from the same field. This means that land preparation must follow harvest very closely, with some work done almost every day. The soil is kept pretty moist for harvest. Two days later it is ideal for tilling.

Santa Ana stolons have been planted into a well-prepared seedbed. After an area of the Santa Ana field is harvested, it is lightly rotary tilled and rolled. If the field needs it, the landplane will be used between rotary tilling and rolling. The bermuda regrows after harvest and does not require replanting.

Soil type

It is not unusual for a sod farm to be located on a soil type that is less that ideal. This comes about as a result of the need to be close to a market, the availability and cost of arable land, and the availability and cost of water. A farm that is already in the family has good availability regardless of the market proximity or soil type.

Sod is grown on muck soils and mineral soils. Mucks are organic soils formed in old bogs, lake beds, and river deltas. Very good sod can be grown on these soils. The soils are very light in weight, so a large quantity can be hauled on a truck. There appears to be little problem with installing muck-grown sod on other soil types. Unfortunately, few sod markets are located near muck soil areas.

Mineral soils are generally formed by the degradation of native rock formations. Wind, water, and alternate heating and cooling break the rock into small fragments, which are classified as sand, silt, and clay particles. The growth of plant life completes the formation of a mineral soil.

The ratio of sand, silt, clay, and organic matter fractions determines the agricultural suitability of these soils. *Loam* soils contain about 40 percent sand, 40 percent silt, and 20 percent clay, and are considered to be the best for growing crops. Ideally, a soil will have at least 5 percent organic matter and 15 percent or less clay. Soils in the southwest seldom have much organic matter content.

Soils that have a little more sand or silt or clay in the ratio are called *sandy loams, silt loams,* or *clay loams.* Sandy loams are preferable to the others. Loam soils drain well, have good moisture-holding capabilities, are easy to work, and are relatively light in weight for transport.

The problem soils are those high in clay content, especially soils with so much clay that they do not fit the loam category: the clay soils. Clay soils do not drain well; they stay wet for long periods. Soil preparation is difficult, and such normal maintenance operations as mowing fall behind because equipment simply cannot be brought into the fields. Many harvest days are lost because of the wet ground. Because these soils hold so much water, they make the sod heavy for hauling.

Most counties in the United States have been surveyed by the Soil Conservation Service (SCS). An SCS map of a given farm will characterize the soil types present. A grower can take a soil sample from a specific field to a local agricultural laboratory and have the soil type determined. Only a few exceptional people can determine a soil type just by feel.

In a soil high in clay content, clods are large and do not readily break up. Soil particles usually are bonded loosely together into aggregates. This aggregation, called the soil structure, is important for air and water movement through the soil. A good soil structure is important for plant growth, because except for pure sand, soil particles are too fine and lay too close together to allow adequate water and air movement. If the soil is too wet, the soil structure can literally be destroyed by tilling, making it nearly impossible to prepare a satisfactory seedbed. If the soil is too dry, the horsepower required to pull preparation equipment through it will be immense and, again, the soil will not break into sufficiently small pieces.

Sometimes sod will develop problems at the interface between the soil on the sod pad and that on the installation site. Such interface problems can prevent rooting. Muck sod and sandy sod have few interface problems, but clay sod can have trouble rooting into sand. Professional turf managers can easily overcome the difficulty, but homeowners are at risk.

Rocky soils are difficult to manage as sod farms. Soil preparation tools such as plowshares, disk blades, and rotary tiller blades are subject to a great deal of abuse in rocky soils, and they quickly wear out. Sod harvesters do not cut the sod cleanly, and their blades dull quickly. Rocky soils greatly increase the costs of maintenance and repair for the harvester.

Soils that have a pH more than a full point on either side of neutral present considerable soil management problems. The pH of a soil is actually a measurement of the hydrogen ions present—a value greater than 7.0 means that the hydrogen ion concentration is lower and the soil is basic (alkaline). A neutral soil has a pH of 7.0. An acid soil has a high concentration of hydrogen ions and a pH of less than 7.0.

A soil of pH 6.0 is 10 times more acidic than a neutral (7.0) soil. Turfgrasses grow quite well in the range between pH 6.0 and pH 7.0. The usual treatment for a pH below 6.0 is to apply lime. Many tons of lime per acre may be needed to bring the pH up to 6.0. The lime application is usually a temporary correction and may have to be repeated every year or two.

An alkaline soil of pH 8.0 is about the most basic in which turfgrasses can be grown. To temporarily correct the pH, growers apply sulfur, often many tons per acre.

A pH in either extreme will make some plant nutrients unavailable to the turfgrass plants. Plant physiology is severely affected by a pH that is out of range.

Soil salinity is a frequent problem in arid climates, and shows up in soil reports as the electroconductivity (ECe) of the soil. An ECe of 4.0 decisiemens (dS) or millimhos (mmho) is the maximum permissible on a sod farm, near to a salinity level that would make it difficult to produce sod at a profit. Turfgrasses can be managed on highly saline soils, but they grow much better on soils of less than 2.0 dS ECe. Excess irrigation can leach the soil and correct any excess soil salinity. The salts wash out of the soil if the water has a lower salinity level than the soil. If the water is more saline than the soil, the field cannot profitably produce sod.

A soil problem sometimes associated with alkalinity and salinity is alkali. An alkali soil is different than an alkaline soil—in the former, sodium is present in a very high concentration. Sodium-affected soils become so tight that water cannot move through. Gypsum applications correct the condition. If there is any choice at all, the sod grower would be better off not trying to grow turf on an alkali soil.

Boron is a problem in arid soils and usually is introduced in the water. Turfgrasses will tolerate relatively higher concentrations of boron than many other crops. Sod has been grown successfully with boron concentrations of 4 parts per million in the soil. If the boron is higher, though, not only can it inhibit turf growth, other arid soil problems are likely to be present, complicating matters.

Soil preparation

Soil preparation is the first cultural practice in sod production and one of the most important. The quality of the work at this stage often determines whether or not a field will be profitable.

To understand why preparation is so vital, just visualize how a sod harvester works. A sod cutter or harvester lifts the turf using a reciprocating blade that slices through the soil just under the grass. The blade is about ½ inch thick, 3 inches from front to back, and 18 inches wide. The working head of the machine rides on a roller, allowing the blade to follow most of the contours of the land. As the unit moves forward, the roller and blade will bridge the little hills, valleys, and holes that are narrower than the width of the blade.

The roller on the cutting head acts as a gauge, allowing the blade to cut at a uniform depth. Surface irregularities left by soil preparation operations cause the cutting head to move erratically, preventing the blade from uniformly cutting the sod.

One low spot a few inches wide will cause a hole in the sod pad, and the entire pad will be thrown away. If the sod is harvested as square-yard pads (9 square feet), one rejected pad in 60 linear feet of harvest will consititute a 10 percent loss. Many of those bad spots can be eliminated right at the beginning, during soil preparation.

The finished sod field must be as flat as the contours of the land will allow. It should look like a vast flat parking lot. No furrows, large or small, can be left by the equipment. Cultipacker rills 1½ inches or less in depth are no problem—the planter will take care of those. The soil should be loose enough to push a shovel into easily, but firm enough to walk on. Some soils, especially those with high silt content, can be over-worked to the point of being powdery. Cultivation should be stopped before the field reaches that stage.

Plowing and disking are farming operations common to many crops. On soils that break up easily (e.g., loams and sandy loams), it may only be necessary to follow the plowing and disking with a cultipacker and landplane. On heavy soils (e.g., clays and clay loams), it may be necessary to follow the disking with a rotary tiller to break up the clods.

Large rotary tillers may replace some of the plowing and disking operations. Loam and sandy loam soils with light moisture can be worked easily and well and are quite conducive to deep rotary tilling. The tilling machines can work a good soil to a depth of 10 to 12 inches. Repeated use of rotary tillers can leave a compacted layer at the working depth, however, so the field should be plowed deep after every third or fourth sod crop to rupture that layer.

The clods of soil should break up pretty uniformly. If 20 percent to 25 percent of the clods are a little larger than 1 inch in diameter and the rest are smaller, they probably will not cause much of a problem, as they will melt with irrigation. The exceptions are the clods that are too hard to melt during the first few irrigations. They may necessitate reworking of the soil after irrigation.

Landplaning is one of the last operations before planting. This is to *true* (flatten) the surface. The field should be planed in several directions to eliminate as many low and high spots as possible. When footprints are more than 1 inch deep in the dry soil, it is too fluffy. This can be remedied by compressing the field with a flat roller. The roller will firm the field without causing excess compaction. If the flat roller is needed, use it after landplaning.

Leveling has become a more important part of agriculture since the development of laser-operated leveling equipment. Most sod fields benefit from laser leveling. The improvement may not be enough to justify the costs, but then again the productivity increase of some fields is dramatic. Surface drainage can improve significantly with the elimination of low spots where water would otherwise accumulate and high spots that would otherwise dry out too quickly.

Fumigating sod fields prior to planting is one of the best ideas to come along since an engine was put on a sod cutter. Most weeds, nematodes, and soilborne diseases can be eliminated by fumigating, as can some insects. Sod quality is improved and crop maturity time is reduced. This operation is common on several high-cash-value crops and, in some markets, these include sod. Fumigate a sod field after harvest and after completing the soil cultivation when the surface is nearly acceptable. It is best if very little work has to be done after a field is fumigated because of the possibility of contamination with new pests.

Three fumigants are commonly used on sod fields: *methyl bromide, chloropicrin,* and *metam-sodium* (Vapam or VPM). Methyl bromide is an odorless, colorless gas that is very effective for weed, insect, and nematode control. Chloropicrin is seldom used alone to fumigate sod fields because it does not control weeds, but it is mixed with methyl bromide to increase the effectiveness of disease control. Even when diseases are not targeted, a small percentage of chloropicrin is often mixed with odorless methyl bromide to provide a warning odor for safety. Chloropicrin is a form of tear gas, so it is easily detected.

Metam-sodium is effective against many of the same pests that methyl bromide and chloropicrin control. Although an excellent fumigant, it has not performed as consistently as the other materials.

Methyl bromide and chloropicrin are injected into the soil as gases, and a plastic tarp is laid on the soil immediately after the injection. Relatively simple machines can inject the fumigants and lay the tarp in one operation. Forty-eight hours later the tarp can be removed and seed can be planted.

Metam-sodium can be sprayed on the soil and irrigated or it can be injected into the irrigation system and applied with the water. Application in the irrigation water is preferable because of the chemical's volatility. In either case, sealing the soil surface with a follow-up irrigation improves effectiveness. The chemical then turns into a gas in the soil. A waiting period of several days must pass for the metam-sodium to dissipate before planting. The big advantage of metam-sodium over the other fumigants is that no tarp is required, but a tarp still improves the effectiveness of the chemical.

For effective fumigation, the soil temperature must be above 55°F in the root zone. Some soil moisture has to be present to aid penetration of fumigants into the weed seeds and into other target organisms, but too much soil moisture will absorb the fumigants and reduce dispersion throughout the soil profile. This is especially significant with the methyl bromide and chloropicrin applications.

Fumigants disappear from the soil very quickly, but by then, pest (insect, disease, weed, and nematode) populations will have been reduced to near eradication. Recurrence of the pest buildup depends upon the sanitation of the sod operation. If irrigation water contains weed seed, as usually happens when the water source is an open canal, or if weeds are permitted to go to seed in the ditches or fencerows, the fumigation will have to be repeated in a short time.

As much of the soil should be fumigated as is possible. Any untreated soil, such as that along ditches, must be avoided by equipment in order to prevent dragging any weeds into the treated field during succeeding soil preparation operations. For example, a landplane can pull untreated soil into the field, leaving large patterns of emerging weeds.

Under normal conditions, the sod grower can expect a fumigation to be effective for 4 to 6 years, sometimes longer, before the pest population builds to problem proportions. Excessive weed invasion is usually the indicator for repeat fumigation. The costs of fumigation, about 2¼ cents per square foot, can be amortized over several crops.

A fertilizer application prior to planting assures that adequate nutrients, especially phosphorus, will be available to the emerging seedlings. A rule of thumb is to apply 500 pounds per acre of 16-20-0 (ammonium phosphate sulphate) or an equivalent. The uniformity of the stand and time to maturity are vastly improved when the nitrogen and phosphorus combination is applied preplant.

Preplant fertilizer is applied even if soil tests show adequate phosphorus. However, soil tests are not to be ignored or discounted—they are indispensable for determining pH and salinity levels and for setting up the crop maintenance nutrition program.

Many sod fields have drainage ditches across the ends or along the sides, so all heavy equipment must turn within the field, often on the turf. This turning will compact the soil and wear the turf out. Twenty to thirty feet at each field end may be lost to harvest, and that can translate to many thousands of square feet of sod. Even though aware of the field-end loss, growers usually plant to the edges of the fields to salvage what they can and to help control dust. Whenever possible, turn equipment on roads or modify ditches by cutting the banks so equipment can cross or turn in them. Lining or paving a gently sloping bank is expensive, but the reduction in sod crop losses may make it economical overall.

Planting

Cool season grasses

Kentucky bluegrass, perennial ryegrass, and tall fescue are the most frequently planted cool season grasses. These grasses are generally planted as seed. The exceptions are a few Kentucky bluegrasses with very good local turf performance characteristics but poor seed production, which are planted vegetatively.

Specific varieties or cultivars (cultivars are "cultivated varieties") of these cool season grasses perform better in some locales than others. Sod growers must select the grasses that will perform best in their particular markets. Seed suppliers and county Cooperative Extension advisors have access to the most recent data on turfgrass variety testing.

Sod growers can purchase *sod-quality seed*, premium seed that has tested for a very high germination percentage and is exceptionally clean, free of weeds, and free of other crop seeds that might otherwise be contaminants. It is expensive, but worth every penny. Seed is still one of the least expensive of all inputs into the crop, and it is foolish to cut corners here. All seed companies that routinely sell to sod growers have sod-quality seed.

Current theory in turfgrass science holds that two or more grasses should be planted together in blends or mixtures. Since each grass responds differently to various stresses, the more tolerant grass will dominate, increasing overall turf performance. A *blend* is the combination of two or more grasses of the same species, such as two Kentucky bluegrasses. A *mixture* is two or more different species combined, such as Kentucky bluegrass and perennial ryegrass.

Blends are usually combined by the seed supplier. Since all the seed

A turfgrass farm field is seeded to a new crop of cool season grass.

is of the same species, seed size will be essentially the same, with little chance of separation. Many suppliers will custom blend for a sod grower due to the large quantities involved.

Mixtures are quite a different story. Since the seed size may differ vastly, there is a chance that mixed seeds will separate by species. The more the seed bags are handled and shaken, the more likely the species will separate, increasing the likelihood that the different grasses will not be distributed uniformly at planting. Even the shaking of the seed box on the planter may be enough to separate the seed.

To overcome the possibility of uneven distribution, growers commonly seed one species first, and then seed the second species over the top of the first. Another technique is to allow the first species to become established, scalp the existing turf, and overseed with the second species. The latter method ensures that the first species will become a significant part of the mixture, especially if there is a big difference in the two species' germination speeds.

In a Kentucky bluegrass–perennial ryegrass mixture, the ryegrass germinates about twice as fast as the bluegrass and has a great deal more seedling vigor. At harvest, bluegrass plants may be difficult to find in the turf, yet the bluegrass will be sufficient to provide sod strength. If Kentucky bluegrass is planted, allowed to become established, and then overseeded with ryegrass, the bluegrass is more likely to be apparent at harvest time.

The seeding rates for cool season grasses vary greatly between climatic regions. In northern areas of the United States, crops often take well over a year to mature. Seeding rates are usually low, 20 to 40 pounds per acre of Kentucky bluegrass. Seeding is usually done in the spring or the fall.

In the sun belt, a crop of cool season grass can mature in as few as 3 months. In these warmer areas, grasses grow almost year round, and sod producers seed Kentucky bluegrass at 80 to 120 pounds per acre. Perennial ryegrasses, when grown by themselves, are seeded at 30 to 50 pounds per acre. The tall fescues are seeded at 200 to 250 pounds per acre and can be forced into a fine texture by seeding at 350 pounds or more per acre. There is some controversy as to whether the very high seeding rates of the tall fescues may cause problems for the consumer, but nothing has been proven one way or the other.

In areas of severe winter temperatures, cool season grasses are seeded either early in the fall or early in the spring. Most growers prefer fall seeding. In the sun belt, grasses are seeded at all times of year. Irrigation after seeding requires a great deal of attention when temperatures exceed 90°F or during periods of dry winds. Water may have to be applied two or three times a day to cool and moisten the soil surface.

Perennial ryegrass-Kentucky bluegrass mixtures should include at least 15 percent but not more than 30 percent perennial ryegrass on a seed-weight basis. If seeded in one application, the seeding rates are 80 to 100 pounds per acre. Even though tall fescues are commonly planted by themselves, mixtures of tall fescue and Kentucky bluegrass are not unusual. These mixtures have 5 to 10 percent Kentucky bluegrass and are seeded at the tall fescue rate. Where established Kentucky bluegrass is to be overseeded with perennial ryegrass to create a mixture, the ryegrass is applied at 80 pounds per acre or more. Some growers use as much as 150 pounds of ryegrass per acre for this kind of overseeding.

The seeder should be carefully calibrated. Poor calibration can cost money and time. An 8-foot seeder pulled 545 feet will cover $\frac{1}{10}$ acre. For an 80-pound-per-acre seeding rate, the seeder would drop 8 pounds of seed. New seeders usually have operator's manuals that include tables of approximate settings for various kinds of seed. A grower can set the seeder according to the book, and knowing the length of the field and the amount of seed left in the hopper, adjust the seeder after the first pass down the field.

Each species is usually seeded in one pass over the field. Some growers prefer to put the seed down one-half at a time. The second pass over the field may be at a right angle to the first. Either way, the operator must constantly watch the seeder to make sure that seed is coming out of all the holes. Looking back at the implement while driving straight is difficult, but it can be done. Turfgrass seeders drop their seed straight down.

Plastic netting can be installed by a rig that rolls it out on top of a seeded field.

The seeder should not overlap the previous pass, but neither should it leave an unplanted gap. The operator must stay alert when seeding.

In the 1970s, plastic netting became important in the production of seeded turfgrass sod. Netted turf can be transplanted and rooted long before it has the mechanical strength to be lifted as sod. Sod strength depends upon rhizomes and tillers—turfgrass roots contribute very little to tensile strength. When the rhizomes and tillers are not fully developed, netting provides that tensile strength. Netting allows the harvest of much younger sod and cuts 25 percent or more from crop maturity time.

The netting can be installed with a machine that seeds, lays netting, and covers both the seed and netting with soil in one operation. This sort of net-laying machine is expensive and slow, but it will prevent several later problems. Wind is a big consideration, and soil-covered netting is little affected by wind. Also, unless the netting is covered, weeds can germinate and push it up in "tents." Another set of problems develops when the planter covers the seed or the netting with too much soil. Seed buried too deep may not germinate. Netting may be buried too deep for the sod cutter blade, and may thus be left in the field, causing a high rate of loss at harvest.

A common way to install netting is to seed first and then simply roll the netting out over the seeded area. This is both the easiest and the least expensive technique. It is also very fast.

Netting in the sod provides the mechanical strength that allows harvest at an early date.

Netting that is rolled out over the surface should be anchored down with wooden sticks, glue, or wire staples to prevent its blowing with the wind, especially if it is laid parallel to the irrigation laterals. If the netting is laid perpendicular to the irrigation laterals, the pipe can serve as the anchor. Except in high wind areas, wooden pegs are probably not needed. Still, the net-laying operation must not get ahead of the pipe, since some netting will move with the slightest breeze until the pipe is put down.

Regardless of how the netting is installed, the growing grass plants will soon secure it to the ground. Even weeds that grow through the mesh will help to lock it down.

Mowers can damage the netting and netting can damage the mowers—both are potential problems. Some netting will stick up above the turf in almost any installation. The mower normally cuts it off and the sweeper picks it up along with the clippings. If the netting catches on the mower and several square feet of netting pull out of the grass, the extracted netting cannot be put back.

Netting does occasionally get wrapped around mower shafts. On reel mowers, wrapped netting will get hot and cause seal failures. On rotary and flail mowers, the netting may bind the blade shafts, and must then be painstakingly removed. Even with these infrequent problems, netting can increase profitability.

The final step in planting cool season grasses is irrigation. Once the seed has been wet, it must be kept moist. In hot weather, the irrigation pattern, wind, and timing will make or break a turfgrass stand. Stand uniformity has a direct relationship to profits.

Warm season grasses

The warm season turfgrasses grown from seed are planted much like the cool season grasses. Most of the newer warm season grasses are planted vegetatively. These either produce seed that has a low germination rate, produce no seed at all, or simply yield poorly.

Preparing soil for vegetative planting is the same as preparation for seeding. The application of preplant fertilizer is also the same.

The most common methods for vegetative planting of turfgrasses are *plugging* and *stolonizing* (sprigging). Essentially, plugs are pieces of sod cut about 2 inches square, with some soil on the roots. The plugs are planted by hand or by machine at a specific spacing (e.g., 12-inch centers). This relatively slow operation is rare on sod farms.

Of the two, the more common method is stolonizing. Stolons are the runners that grow above the ground and allow certain grasses to spread. Harvested stolons, in different markets, are either called stolons or sprigs. Along the length of the stolon are several joints, or nodes. Each node contains a bud capable of growing a new plant exactly like the parent. Ideally, stolons would be harvested and cut into sections, each section bearing a single node. This technique is possible, but economically impractical.

To harvest stolons, growers chop turf into small pieces. The intent is to strip away the stolons, leaving all the roots and soil behind. Commercial sprig-harvesting machines do a very good, efficient job, cutting the stolons into uniform lengths and separating the soil from the plant material. Producing stolons for sale can be a lucrative sideline for a sod grower.

Sod growers who want to expand their stoloniferous grass acreage can take advantage of some simple harvest methods. These techniques are labor intensive and they provide stolons that are adequate for internal use, but not uniform enough for commercial sale. One method is to let the turf go unmowed for a time. This increases the number of stolons and tends to prevent many of them from contacting the soil. A forage harvester can be run over the area and the plant material collected in a bin or trailer.

By knowing the volume of the bin or trailer, the grower can estimate the number of bushels available for planting. Unfortunately, a bushel of stolons has not been well defined. The grower can either consider 2 cubic feet (approximately 8 pounds) of stolons or the stolons harvested from 1 square yard of turf to be a bushel.

The objective in planting stolons is to distribute the stolons uniformly and cover them with soil. Stolon-planting machines are available and hydromulching machines have been used successfully to plant stolons.

Hybrid bermudagrass is planted as stolons.

Growers planting their own stolons can spread them by hand or with a manure spreader and then run over them with a light disk or a culti-packer. More than one pass over the area may be necessary. Disk blades should be set straight (closed) to prevent the normal soil-turning action. Stolons buried deeper than 2 inches probably will not survive.

Planting rates for stolons vary depending upon the grass and the speed of turf coverage desired. A practical and economical planting rate is 200 bushels per acre. For planning purposes, estimate that the quantity of stolons harvested from an area of a given size will plant an area 20 times that size.

Many of the warm season grasses used in sod production will regrow without being replanted. Those with rhizomes (something like an underground stolon) can be harvested cleanly as sod without leaving narrow strips (*ribbons*) to grow back. These grasses (e.g., bermudagrasses and zoysiagrasses) will grow back from the rhizomes left below the harvester's blade. Rotary tilling can smooth the field, removing ruts made during the sod harvest operation.

The sod of stoloniferous grasses that do not have rhizomes (e.g., St. Augustinegrass) is harvested in a way that leaves ribbons of turf in the field. These can then be allowed to spread and fill the intervening spaces or rotary tilled to distribute stolons. Rotary tilling also smoothes the field. If no ribbons are left, the field will have to be replanted.

Many fields are smoothed by landplaning and then rolling with a flat roller, just as in preplanting soil preparation. Too much waste or other debris in the field can make landplaning more of a trouble than it is worth. Simply rolling in such a case will be helpful. If ribbons are left in the field, rolling is about the only smoothing method that can be used. Preplant fertilizer is applied after smoothing.

Irrigation is the most important single factor in successful stolon planting. Since they are planted into dry soil, stolons dry out very quickly. On a hot day, an hour may be too long to wait before getting water on the planting. It is critical to plant no more than can easily be irrigated. Hold the stolons in bags or bins and sprinkle them frequently to keep them moist and cool, rather than plant them and then not get the water on fast enough. The most common cause of stolon planting failure is improper watering.

Except in tropical and subtropical climates, warm season grasses should not be planted after September 15. There have been many successful plantings later in the year, but the risk is very high. For spring planting, soil temperatures should be consistently above 55°F.

Overseeding and winter color

Turfgrass growers overseed sod for three reasons: to mix grasses, to improve a stand, and to provide winter color. Mixing grasses would be something like overseeding an established stand of Kentucky bluegrass with perennial ryegrass. This combines the sod strength of bluegrass with the disease resistance of ryegrass.

If a stand of tall fescue is not uniform, it can be improved by over-seeding with the same cultivar of tall fescue. The field will not mature as originally planned, but more of it will be available for eventual harvest.

Warm season grasses tend to go dormant and turn brown in the winter. Overseeding with a cool season species is a common practice on fine turf areas such as golf courses, since it helps maintain a green turf year round. The overseeded grass is expected to disappear when summer temperatures get high. Few sod farms overseed for winter color, but some markets demand it.

An alternative to overseeding for winter color is to apply a colorant. Turf colorants are dyes or paints that adhere to dead tissue. The colorant is diluted in water and applied with an agricultural sprayer. It is sprayed, allowed to dry, then sprayed again. The grower repeats the process until the color is as desired. Skilled application will yield a very natural-looking turf.

Because the colorants are really paints, they will adhere to nearly anything—concrete walks, pipe, equipment, trees, clothing, and build-ings included. Once dry, they pose no threat to clothing or shoes. Even though they may not routinely stock colorants, turf chemical and fertilizer suppliers can obtain them from manufacturers.

When overseeding turfgrass for sod, the turf is "scalped" by very low mowing. Vertical mowing can reduce the sod strength and should be avoided. The seed is applied at the chosen rate.

After overseeding, drag the field with a length of chainlink fence or something similar to shake the seed down into the mat. Irrigation should be such that the surface will not dry out for the first week. This may require irrigation two or three times per day. The new seed is lying uncovered on the surface and is very susceptible to drying out and dying. Even at that, only a small percentage of the seed will germinate, and this is the reason for the heavy seeding rate. Water management is the key to suc-cessful overseeding.

The species used for winter color overseeding are annual ryegrass, perennial ryegrass, red fescue, chewings fescue, and *Poa trivialis*. The ryegrasses and fescues are seeded at 300 to 600 pounds per acre. *Poa trivialis* is seeded at 120 to 150 pounds per acre (use *Poa annua*-free seed to avoid future problems with that weed).

In most of the sun belt, winter color can also be forced by using a plastic tarp. Many sports fields use this technique through the football season.

The plastic tarp must be at least 4 mills thick, but a 10-mill tarp is best. The tarp must have ventilation, which is provided by punching ½-inch diameter holes on 6-inch centers. The ventilation prevents excess heat buildup. Soil temperatures can be raised 5° to 7°F, often enough to prevent dormancy. The same technique is used to germinated seed in cold soils. It is quite expensive, so its usefulness is limited on sod farms.

Turnaround

The next step after harvest is preparing and planting the newly harvested field. The grower's goal should be to turn a field around as quickly as is practical, starting irrigation on the new planting within 3 weeks of removal of the last harvested sod.

To do this, the grower must perform all necessary plowing and disking as the field is harvested. Soil moisture will be good at that time, and a big part of the soil preparation will be underway. The tractor drivers must not get too close to the harvesters, though, or there will be no room for the delivery trucks and forklifts.

The normal soil preparation and planting operations follow, and the cycle begins again. It is important that the seed be ordered, delivered, and in the barn when it is needed.

5

Growing

Eucre Sod

Eucre Sod has good-quality water pumped from its own well. For establishment of the turf, the company has enough solid set aluminum pipe with sprinklers to irrigate 50 acres. When turfgrasses no longer require frequent irrigation, the solid-set pipe is removed and movable wheel lines are put in a field. Each wheel line can irrigate about 10 acres.

The water well production is sufficient to allow Eucre Sod to run six solid-set lines and four wheel lines at the same time. Watering must be scheduled with that in mind. There are 12 valve openers for the solid set. While six valves run for a 1-hour set, another six lines can be moved and hooked up. Little time will be lost turning off the first six lines and turning on the next six.

Wheel lines must be drained before before being moved from one valve to the next. It takes 20 minutes to drain a wheel line and a total of 20 minutes for the irrigator to walk to the mover, move the line, walk back to the valve, hook up the line, and pressurize the system. The line can be unhooked while it is draining. A 1-hour irrigation set requires 1 hour and 40 minutes.

There are nine mainline valves per 10 acres (actually 10.8 acres). It will take about 14½ hours to irrigate the 10 acres (eight valves times 1 hour and 40 minutes plus one hour for the ninth), not including the 40 minutes needed to drain and move the last set.

A minimum of nearly 2 working days or 2 shifts must be spent to irrigate the 10 acres once, so stretching the expected number of acres per wheel line is imprudent. In hot weather, the turf may not be able to go more than 2 days between irrigations without yielding an economic loss at harvest time.

A 1-hour set on either type of Eucre Sod irrigation system will apply 0.4 inches of water. The new seedings and very young grass are watered as frequently as necessary to keep the soil surface moist. Established fields are irrigated according to evapotranspiration (ET) information supplied from a nearby California Irrigation Management Information System (CIMIS) station. Irrigators have been taught to use the ET data to schedule irrigation, but also to be aware of weather changes such as rain or dry winds that would require application of more or less water.

Fields of Eucre Sod's Elite tall fescue blend are mowed to 1½ inches year round. The turf could grow to 2¼ inches before mowing. If it takes 2 weeks to grow to 2¼ inches, that is the mowing schedule. If it takes only 5 days, as it does in the spring, that becomes the mowing schedule. Fields are swept after each mowing and the clippings disposed of at an on-farm dump site.

Eucre Sod mows the Santa Ana to ⅝ inch. It is always mowed before it grows to 1 inch. The frequency of mowing is determined by the growth rate, just as is the Elite mowing schedule. In the summer, Santa Ana grows fast, and often has to be mowed twice a week.

Fumigation and frequent replanting help prevent pest population build-up, so pest control is not a big problem at Eucre Sod. When any disease, insect, or weed becomes a problem, the treatment follows University of California recommendations. Fortunately, Santa Ana is resistant to most diseases and insects because it seldom is replanted. If a pest population does build to a problem level, the affected area is fumigated and replanted with stolons from a clean area of the field. If there were no clean areas, new stolons would have to be purchased.

Most of the soils in the Eucre Sod market area are similar to that of the farm. In areas where there is a potential problem with the interface of the soil on the sod and that on the installation site, the company works with the customer to setting up cultural practices that will alleviate the situation.

The process of growing turfgrass sod includes irrigation, mowing, plant nutrition, and pest control. These are simultaneous operations, and poor execution of any one of them will have a direct impact upon profit.

The use of netting on cool season grasses has significantly reduced the needed growing time. Before netting, there may have been sufficient time to overcome mistakes in irrigation, mowing, or fertilization. With netting, there is no time to recover from such errors. This puts a great deal of pressure on production personnel and management.

Irrigation

Growing turfgrass sod in arid climates makes irrigation absolutely the most important operation in the production cycle. Getting the maximum efficiency out of the irrigation system and the water application is a full-time job.

Irrigation systems employed on sod farms are most often adapted from those developed for general agriculture, rather than the sophisticated, permanently installed equipment widely used on large turf installations. Permanently installed turfgrass management systems consist of controllers, buried lines, automatic valves, and pop-up sprinklers. They are expensive but efficient systems.

Irrigation systems

On sod farms, one must consider the capital investment in the irrigation system. Arguments can be made for long-term returns on an investment in the automatic systems, but sod growers are often on leased land. Even on their own land, they are reluctant to commit the funds needed to install such a system on several hundred acres. Also, problems are likely when sod cutters and land preparation equipment work over and around the sprinklers.

Irrigation systems on sod farms use portable pipe or movable structures that allow work to go on in the fields. Even though automatic clocks and valves are available for use on portable systems, most require tending. Many require that an irrigator turn the water on and off at the desired running time.

Sod growers use solid-set aluminum irrigation pipe. It is labor intensive to move, but good for "on-demand" water on new plantings. Sideways-moving wheel lines, laterally moving tower structures, and center pivots are all used successfully to produce turfgrass sod. Irrigation equipment is discussed more thoroughly in the Appendix.

Scheduling

The irrigator may be the most important employee in the company. He or she must be dependable, hard working, capable of making decisions, and skilled in the management of water. The irrigator's actions can cost or save the company huge sums of money.

It would be impractical to have a water supply, pumps, and mainline sufficient to run all of the sprinklers at the same time. Therefore, the supply must be balanced between the various fields so turf plantings in several stages of maturity will receive the correct amount of water. Too little water will stress the grass. Too much water can injure the turf, leach nutrients, and increase costs unnecessarily by wasting water.

Here is one example of water waste. The sprinklers in a field apply 0.5 acre-inch per hour, there are 100 acres in turf, and the water costs $240 per acre-foot ($20 per acre-inch). If the irrigation were 1 hour per acre per week more than needed, the loss would be

$$0.5 \text{ acre-in/hr} \times 1 \text{ hr/wk} \times 100 \text{ acres} \times \$20/\text{acre-in} = \$1,000/\text{wk}.$$

This kind of waste can easily happen with three irrigation sets per week if the irrigator gets behind. The average of 20 minutes' extra watering on each field can be hard to notice.

A newly planted field will need water every day, at least, and may have to be irrigated more than once a day. A 6-week-old field may require irrigation every other day, and a mature field every third day. The water delivery must keep these individual water regimes in balance.

A harvest field must receive water the night before harvest, but not so much as to render it muddy or sloppy the next day. Fertilizer, iron, and pesticide applications may have to be watered in to prevent burn or to activate the material. Mowers can only work on fields that have dried enough to prevent rutting. Irrigation needs do not stop on the weekends or holidays, so someone must cover those periods. Irrigation scheduling impacts the entire production operation.

A useful tool in irrigation management is the soil probe. This is a slotted tube that can be stuck into the soil to remove a small sample. The observer can see to what depth the soil is dry or wet—there is no guessing. Data from the probe can be used in scheduling. If the soil is dry after 4 days, irrigation may be needed every 3 days. A more sophisticated tool for irrigation scheduling is the measurement of evapotranspiration.

Several soil moisture sensing devices are on the market. Tensiometers are among the most common. They measure the suction created by drying soil. These instruments have gauges that can be read every day or connected to automatic reporting instruments. Automatic irrigation systems on golf courses often use tensiometers to turn sprinklers on and off. Other moisture-sensing devices usually measure electrical conductivity in a moisture-absorbing porous block or membrane. Any of these can be a valuable tool, correctly used.

Turfgrass roots do not run deep. Established, mature turf has roots 2 or more feet deep, but the immature turf in sod production has most of its roots near the soil surface. Irrigation only has to moisten a soil profile of about 4 to 8 inches, or at most 1 foot. This means there is no big reservoir from which the plant can draw moisture. That shallow profile must be replenished frequently.

Wheel-line irrigation is one good method of watering a growing field of turf.

Sod irrigation usually puts water on as fast as the soil will take it, as frequently as necessary. Irrigation sets seldom last longer than 1 hour. A set is the length of time the irrigation runs in one spot. In general agriculture, sets commonly run as long as 24 hours, with a low water application rate to wet a deep soil profile. Such a set repeats every 2 or 3 weeks. A small quantity of pipe can thus irrigate many acres because there is plenty of time to move it to the next set. But the sod irrigator, irrigating every 2 or 3 days, does not have time to move the pipe very far.

On some sod farms, because of their unique situations, water is cheap. With the lower water cost, those companies can have a competitive advantage in pricing. Turfgrass sod is a good crop to irrigate with inexpensive, treated effluent water. However, the grower must be aware of the chemical content of the effluent water; dissolved salts, boron, certain metals, and other constituents can be in concentrations high enough to harm turf. For many growers, water is expensive and must be carefully managed to control production costs.

Evapotranspiration

Cool season grasses require between 3.3 and 4 acre-feet of water per acre per year for sod production. Warm season grasses require between 2.5 and 3.3 acre-feet per acre per year. Most of that water is supplied as

Another method is solid-set portable pipe irrigation, which also gives the uniform field coverage necessary for a newly planted turf crop.

irrigation from April through October. In the winter months, rainfall supplements the irrigation. The water requirements are the same whether supplied by irrigation or rainfall.

One acre-foot is the amount of water required to cover 1 acre of land 1 foot deep, approximately 325,900 gallons. An acre-inch is one-twelfth of an acre-foot. The cost of 1 acre-foot of irrigation water varies from $30 to over $400. A sod producer could spend over $1,600 per acre on water to grow a crop of a cool season grass. Since field losses and waste will keep the grower from selling all of the sod he or she grows, the cost of water per acre of actual sales can be substantially greater than $1,600.

On 20 acres' production, the grower would spend $32,000 for water. With losses and waste of 10 percent (a good percentage), 18 acres would be sold. The water cost per sales acre would then be $1,778.

The rate of water use actually depends upon evapotranspiration (ET), the combined amount of water lost to the atmosphere from evaporation and transpired to the atmosphere by plants. For practical purposes, ET is the amount of water a turfgrass crop uses, and is measured in inches per unit of time. It is a very useful tool in irrigation management. For example: ET is 0.25 inches per day in June (30 days), there are 100 acres of turf, and water costs $240 per acre-foot or $20 per acre-inch. The June water bill would be forecast as

$$0.25 \text{ ET(acre-in/day)/acre} \times 30 \text{ days} \times 100 \text{ acres} \times \$20/\text{acre-in} = \$15,000.$$

Evapotranspiration is particularly useful in the design of an irrigation system for which the crop's needs can be estimated accurately. The irrigation system would simply have to be capable of applying the ET of the highest-use period.

Computerized weather stations report ET for various climatic zones in several states. In California, CIMIS provides local ET figures for growers located throughout the state. Commercial irrigation manufacturers are marketing the stations for use on specific sites. The stations are valuable for scheduling irrigation by the water budgeting method.

The weather station reports the amount of ET over a given period of time. Irrigation is then scheduled to replace the amount of water lost or used. This is a relatively simple approach, but in practice it does require good management and efficient irrigation equipment.

County Cooperative Extension offices can provide information about where to get ET data. For more information about using ET and irrigation design refer to *Turfgrass Water Conservation*, Publication 21405.

Uniformity

The uniform distribution of water is a key factor in producing quality sod. The design of the system and the condition of irrigation equipment are critical. If either is poor, there is little chance of success. If both are good, uniformity will depend upon the people operating the system.

Design involves matching (1) the amount of water available with (2) the pressure to the sprinklers, lateral pipes, and mainlines, and (3) the spacing of all of them, while considering (4) the needs of the crop, (5) the prevailing winds, and (6) other local conditions. These problems are handled best by an irrigation designer or engineer. Most reputable, established irrigation supply companies either have personnel capable of this type of design or can recommend local designers.

The pumps, valves, pipelines, and sprinklers must be in good repair. Inefficient pumps, leaky valves, and pipes in poor condition affect pressure and volume. The local power company will test an electric pump for its operating efficiency at little or no cost. Pump companies will test engine-driven pumps at minimal cost. If the pumps are on wells, testing will include the static water level and the drawn-down level, which together indicate the condition of the well. Periodic testing of pumps can help prevent maintenance problems.

Worn nozzles and sprinkler parts cause erratic irrigation patterns. Bent impact arms, frozen gear boxes, and broken impellers can turn good sod to waste. Because they are generally so dependable, it is easy to forget that sprinklers need maintenance just like any other equipment.

One of the biggest problems when using older irrigation systems is the mixture of sprinklers or nozzles. All of the nozzles in the system, at least in a given field, must be of the same size. Different brands or sizes of sprinklers will cause variations in water distribution. Amazingly, it is not unusual to find different-sized nozzles in a sod field operated by a grower who knows better. These things tend to slip by, yet must not.

Drought stress

Wilting turf is the first symptom of drought stress. The grass has a gray-blue patina that is seen easily from some distance. Up close, the turf readily shows footprints, since the grass blades tend to not spring back up after they are compressed. In the early stages of stress, the turf will recover with immediate water application. As wilt progresses, the blades may die, but the turf will recover even though its growth is temporarily retarded. If drought continues, turf plants will die, and the density of the planting will decline. A severe drought area usually does not recover enough to be harvested with the rest of the field, and it ultimately becomes waste. Seemingly minor drought stress of the turfgrass can cause heavy waste at harvest, weeks or even months later.

Drought stress seldom occurs uniformly over a field. Normally, there are distinct patterns of stress that conform to irrigation or soil variations. It is impossible to apply water perfectly, so some areas will always receive more or less water than others. Soils may vary a great deal throughout a field. Heavy clays that stay wet can be found beside sandy areas that do not hold moisture. Poorly designed or operated irrigation systems magnify these differences.

Drought patterns in the shapes of circles, rings, triangles, or strips show that something is wrong with the irrigation system. Too low or too high a pressure, plugged sprinklers, sprinklers cocked at an angle, and broken sprinklers could be causes. Laterals that are too far apart will leave strips of stressed turf. Any of these could be the fault of the design, the system maintenance, or the way the irrigator has laid out the sprinklers. But nature does not work in regular patterns like humans do. Regular patterns mean system problems.

If the soil is the problem, the drought pattern will not correspond to the irrigation system. Irregular patterns may correspond to the slope of the land, knolls, swales, or some other readily visible factor. The cause may be hard to detect. A laboratory soil analysis may be required to determine the source of the drought stress problem.

The irrigation of turfgrasses for sod production remains more an art than a science. Weather, soil, species, and equipment make the application of water an operation unique to each sod farm.

Mowing

Mowing grass is about the most common, routine task in turf growing. It is also one of the biggest costs of sod production. Mowing can develop and maintain turf quality, and can get the sod crop to mature on time.

If the turf is allowed to grow too tall and is cut back excessively, the growth rate is significantly slower. The rule of thumb is to cut off no more than one-third of the leaf length at any one mowing. This is sometimes easier to say than to accomplish, especially in the spring. At that time, growth is so fast that it is difficult for a grower to keep up. Also, in many areas, spring rains can keep the ground too wet to support the mower's weight without damage, and this can disrupt mowing schedules and allow the grass to outgrow the mowing.

Mowing height and frequency

If the grass is more than one and one-third times its normal mowing height, the mower should be set to one-third the length of the grass blades, and then lowered over several mowings. This will keep shock to the plants at a minimum. This technique is inconvenient, nearly impractical, and always good for an argument from employees, but it protects profits. The exceptions are some of the warm season grasses (e.g., bermudagrasses) that can be scalped down quickly and will recover with little observable effect.

Cool season grasses such as Kentucky bluegrass, perennial ryegrass, and tall fescue are mowed to 1½ to 2 inches. The higher end of the range is better when the temperatures are above 90°F. As harvest nears, these grasses should be maintained as short as practical to maintain a better product appearance. Never mow them lower than 1¼ inches.

Measure the mowing height on a reel mower from a flat surface, such as a concrete floor, to the top of the bedknife. On a rotary mower, measure it from a flat floor to the bottom of the cutting blade.

Hybrid bermudagrasses are maintained at ½ to ⅝ inch. At this mowing height the grasses scalp easily, mostly due to irregularities in the soil surface. Two to three weeks before harvest, the mower should be raised ¹⁄₁₆ to ⅛ inch, if practical. This small increase in height can make the difference between green sod and brown, scalped sod. In some operations, it is very difficult to change the mowing height for the harvest material and then to lower it back for the rest of the bermuda.

St. Augustinegrass should be maintained at about 1 inch. Most zoysiagrasses are satisfactory if mowed to ⅝ or 1 inch. Seashore *paspalum* is fine if mowed the same as the hybrid bermudagrasses. A good dichondra sod product is mowed at 1 inch.

Mowing frequency can be determined according to the rule of thumb. For example, a grass that is mowed to 1½ inches should be mowed before it exceeds 2¼ inches, and a grass that is mowed to ⅝ inch should be mowed before it exceeds 1 inch. If that growth occurs in 3 days, then the field should be mowed every 3 days or so; if it takes 2 weeks, then that should be the mowing frequency.

A well-maintained reel mower will give the cleanest, best-looking cut.

Mower operation

Mowers are big, heavy pieces of equipment. If the soil is too wet, these machines can make ruts in the field. Ruts will cause harvest losses that might have been avoided.

To maximize sod quality, use a reel mower on all grasses as harvest nears. This is especially necessary for the last four or five mowings, regardless of the type of mower normally used. There is no cut comparable to that of a sharp, properly adjusted reel mower, and the quality of the final product can definitely be increased. Mowers and other equipment are more thoroughly discussed in the Appendix.

Regardless of the type of mower, maintain the blades well and keep them sharp. Dull blades leave the grass tips frayed and bruised. Frayed tips dry out, leaving brown tissue, slowing growth (especially in hot weather), and reducing turf quality.

Problems can occur when the same mowers are used for several different grasses. On low-mowed, warm season grasses, cut stolons often catch on the mower. These become a source of contamination. A mower should be thoroughly washed after leaving a warm season grass field and before entering a field with any other kind of grass, even another cultivar of the same species (e.g., going from Tifgreen bermuda to Santa Ana bermuda).

Mowing is a repetitive, boring job. There is a tendency for the operator to go too fast in order to get done. Driving too fast causes the mower to bounce, giving an irregular cut and putting great stress on the decks, blades, reels, and drive units. This is also how mowers run into things, such as sprinkler equipment, ditches, or anything else in or close to the field.

Dew may cover the grass in the early mornings, and wet grass is difficult to mow. Usually, it is possible to wait until midmorning for the dew to burn off before starting to mow. On overcast days, the dew either will burn off much later or will not burn off at all. It may be necessary to mow anyway in order to keep from getting too far behind.

When mowing wet turf, clippings accumulate on the mower wheels and the rollers that serve as the cutting height gauges. The operator must stop occasionally and clean them to protect the mowing quality and the equipment. Clippings can build up to the point that they will prevent rollers and reels from turning.

Wet clippings fall from the mower in clumps. These clumps cannot be left on the turf more than a couple of days or they will kill the grass beneath them.

Clippings

Not all growers pick up grass clippings. In areas where sod can be produced in less than a year, clippings are usually removed. When the turf is long or wet, clippings will lie on top, usually in clumps, and can kill the grass in spots. If not lying on top, the clippings filter down into the turf and turn brown. When the sod is delivered it may appear to have less density than it really has. As far as the customer is concerned, such sod is not of good quality.

Sweepers and vacuums are used to pick up the clippings, and both operate more slowly than mowers. The equipment must be transported to a dump site, the clippings unloaded, and the equipment transported back to the field. Even if the dump site is close to the field, the round trip can easily take 30 to 40 minutes. Disposal trips are frequent, since most sweepers and vacuums have relatively small hoppers to keep them from becoming too heavy. Thus, clipping removal takes a great deal of time.

Clipping disposal is a big problem. Sod farms generate many tons of the material, and it accumulates in large, unsightly piles. The piles become a smelly breeding place for flies and other insects.

When set afire, clipping piles burn very slowly and produce a lot of smoke. This sort of burning is illegal in most communities. Clippings make poor compost and poor land fill, and because of pesticide use they are not satisfactory for livestock feed. Some innovative growers have developed methods to utilize clippings, but most just wish they would go away.

Clippings of low-mowed grasses often contain stolon pieces. The stolons can then contaminate other grasses. Great care should be taken when handling bermuda and zoysia clippings. Wind can distribute the clippings and stolons over a wide area including nearby tall fescue or Kentucky bluegrass fields.

After mowing, a tractor-towed vacuum can remove grass clipping from the field.

Plant nutrition

Turfgrasses are actually being forced to produce their maximum growth rate for sod production. Even though sod is sold on the basis of the quality and appearance of the verdure—the green foliage left on the plant after mowing—the grower must be sure it is balanced with root and rhizome development.

Growth response

The shoots and roots of turfgrass plants grow at different rates, the shoots growing much faster. If the shoots grow so fast that the root structure cannot support the growth, carbohydrate reserves will deplete, and the plants may fall victim to disease and stress.

If the shoots grow too slowly, insufficient photosynthetic material will be available to sustain the root growth, carbohydrates will not be produced in adequate amounts, density will be reduced, the turf will weaken, and the plants may fall victim to disease and stress.

The ideal ratio of growth rates for turfgrass sod shoots and roots is about 7:1. The fertilizer program for sod production should get maximum growth while maintaining that shoot-to-root ratio. Obviously, it is im-

A broadcast spreader applies fertilizer to a turfgrass field.

practical for a grower to go into the field and determine the sod's shoot-to-root ratio in order to set up a fertilizer program. The recommendations drawn from regular soil testing can help a grower keep the nutrients in balance.

The optimum soil temperature for the growth of cool season grass shoots ranges from 65° to 80°F. For the roots, the soil temperature range is 55° to 65°F, measured 6 inches deep. The optimum soil temperatures for warm season grass shoots range from 80° to 95°F, and 70° to 80°F for the roots. When the temperature goes above the optimum rate for the roots, growth slows, but the growth of shoots increases at the same time.

A daily record of soil temperatures is easy to maintain and follow with a recording thermometer. If the trend of the soil temperatures moves up to or through the optimum range for the roots, fertilizer applications can help get the maximum benefit from the conditions. If the soil temperature trend is above the optimum, a fertilizer application will have a negative effect on the turf by further stimulating shoot growth. If the soil temperature trend is lower than the optimum range, a fertilizer application would likely be wasted on the slow-growing turf.

That is a useful approach to growing sod, but turf may also need fertilizer to improve its color during hot weather. If the night air temperatures cool down into the 60s, the adverse effect on the grass will be greatly decreased. If night temperatures stay in the 80s or 90s, a fertilizer application is almost sure to cause problems.

Nitrogen, phosphorus, and potassium (NPK)

The turfgrass plant requires nitrogen (N), phosphorus (P), and potassium (K) in relatively large quantities. In addition, several minor elements are required for plant growth. The minor element most frequently found deficient is iron (Fe). Soil testing is a valuable way to determine the availability of these nutrients.

All fertilizer labels have three numbers to indicate the percentage by weight of nitrogen, phosphorus, and potassium, respectively. If one of these elements is absent from the fertilizer, there will be a zero in that nutrient's place. Nutrients are usually recommended by pounds per acre or pounds per 1,000 square feet of the actual nutrient. When nitrogen is present, the amount of fertilizer is calculated by the rate of nitrogen needed. Fertilizer is calculated as

$$\frac{\text{lb of nitrogen/acre}}{\% \text{ nitrogen in fertilizer}} \times 100 = \text{lb of fertilizer/acre}$$

For example: If 40 pounds of N per acre are recommended and the fertilizer is ammonium sulfate (21-0-0), calculate $^{40}/_{21} \times 100 = 190.5$ pounds of ammonium sulfate per acre.

Nitrogen is extensively used by the plant. It is easily lost to the atmosphere and easily leached by irrigation water, so it must be applied regularly. The availability of nitrogen to the plant is difficult to determine by laboratory diagnostic techniques. Nitrogen recommendations for sod are based more upon general rules for the turf species, time of year, and soil type.

The standard recommendation for nitrogen fertilizer is 40 pounds of actual nitrogen per acre per month of growing season on most cool season turfgrasses grown for sod. To maintain color during the winter in the sun belt, the grower might use 60 pounds of actual nitrogen per acre per month.

On warm season grasses, 80 pounds of soluble nitrogen per acre in early spring, just as the plants are coming out of dormancy, helps get them off and running. As the temperatures reach optimum levels, these grasses readily respond to nitrogen applications of 40 pounds per acre per month.

Even when the temperatures go over the optimum, there is little danger of adversely affecting the roots of warm season grasses with soluble nitrogen applications. As temperatures move below the optimum, dormancy can often be delayed with soluble nitrogen applications, even when soil temperatures dip to the lower 50s.

Any application of soluble nitrogen as high as 80 pounds per acre to cool season grasses during the normal growing season will cause excess shoot growth, and the grasses will require more frequent mowing and have an unfavorable shoot-to-root ratio. As soil temperatures move above the optimum range, nitrogen applications should stop. Cool season grasses are extremely susceptible to stress in the presence of excess nitrogen at high temperatures.

If the grower is interested in clipping yield as opposed to sod production, Kentucky bluegrass will respond with increasing levels of nitrogen up to about 130 pounds of nitrogen per acre per month. However, economic returns on the fertilizer inputs generally top out between 40 and 80 pounds of nitrogen per acre per month in the growing season. This readily shows up as a decrease in clipping yields when nitrogen applications exceed 40 pounds per acre in warm weather.

Phosphorus is required for various functions in the plant. Among the most important for the sod grower are the root growth and rhizome development. Phosphorus is generally listed on the fertilizer bag as the equivalent to P_2O_5 (in this context, "P" signifies the P_2O_5 equivalent).

Even though soil tests may indicate sufficient phosphorus availability, there are advantages to having excess P present for new seedlings. A preplant application of 500 pounds of 16-20-0 per acre makes N and excess P immediately available to the rapidly growing seedlings, and this availability makes an obvious difference in stand development. The same response is evident in new plantings of stolonized warm season grasses. If the soil tests indicate adequate phosphorus, there is no general advantage to applying additional phosphorus for the rest of the sod crop cycle.

Potassium is seldom deficient on soils in the western United States. Soil tests will show potassium availability, and if applications are necessary they can be made according to the recommendations in the test report. To keep the record straight, potassium is listed on the fertilizer bag as the K_2O equivalent. Most literature shows "K" to represent the K_2O equivalent.

N sources

Nitrogen is sold for fertilizer in various forms. The more common soluble forms are urea (45-0-0), ammonium sulfate (21-0-0), ammonium nitrate (33-0-0), and calcium nitrate (15-0-0). In these forms, nitrogen is quickly available to the plants, which should respond in only 2 or 3 days. On a per-unit of nitrogen basis, they are the least expensive forms. The disadvantage to these materials is that they do not last very long. The turf will begin to show deficiency in a little over 1 month.

Five sources of slow-release nitrogen fertilizers are readily available. The per-unit of nitrogen cost for each is much greater than for the solubles, but the slow-release forms last for 2 to 3 months. Organic fertilizers such as manures and activated sewage sludge are low in nitrogen and generally unsuited for sod production, although some soils have shown significant improvements with very large manure applications.

Nitrogen in ureaform (ureaformaldehyde) is released by soil microorganisms. It is very effective, but the release is slowed when cool soil temperatures reduce the activity of the microorganisms. Isobutylidine diurea (IBDU) is released as it slowly dissolves in soil moisture. The size of the IBDU particle determines the length of time the material will last, larger particles lasting longer. As long as the soil temperature remains above freezing, it will not affect IBDU.

Two of the slow-release nitrogen sources are coated materials. The effective release rate of sulfur-coated urea (SCU) and resin-coated fertilizers depend upon the thickness and porosity of the coating. Resin-coated fertilizers are not limited to nitrogen; the resin can coat almost any nutrient the manufacturer chooses. The advantage of these materials is that the release rate can be controlled fairly precisely by the design of the coating.

P sources

Phosphorus is available as single super phosphate (0-18-0) or triple super phosphate (0-45-0). Since a nitrogen supplement is nearly always needed, growers commonly use one fertilizer containing both nitrogen and phosphorus. Ammonium phosphate-sulfate is the 16-20-0 fertilizer used most often by sod growers. The second most common fertilizer is monoammonium phosphate (11-48-0).

Iron

Plants use iron in the formation of chlorophyll. When iron is deficient, grass plants become chlorotic. First the younger leaves turn yellow, showing up in irregular patches in the field. In contrast, nitrogen deficiency first becomes evident on the older leaves and is more uniform throughout a sod field.

The most likely soils for iron deficiency are calcareous, high pH, sandy, or cold and wet. The severity of iron chlorosis increases with the excessive shoot production associated with spring growth and high nitrogen fertilization. Calcareous soils are high in calcium carbonate or lime and have a characteristic pH of 8.0 or more. The presence of so much calcium makes the iron chemically unavailable to the plant.

A plant's soil may contain iron that is unavailable to the plant. An alkaline pH of over 7.0 will keep much of the iron tied up. The pH can be lowered with annual applications of sulfur at 100 to 200 pounds of elemental sulfur per acre, and this can help release the iron. Calcareous soils are corrected in the same manner.

Soils naturally resist changes in pH through the chemical activity known as *buffering*. The pH of a highly buffered soil will be very difficult to lower. Of the three sulfur materials—elemental sulfur, sulfuric acid, and ferrous sulfate—ferrous sulfate has the least effect on pH, but it contains iron and will help darken the color of the turf.

Several iron products are used to relieve iron deficiency. Ferrous sulfate, the most common and usually the least expensive, contains 21 percent iron. Ferrous sulfate is the quickest-acting material; it improves turf color within a couple of days, but the improvement does not last long. Applications of 20 to 40 pounds of elemental iron (about 100 to 200 lb of ferrous sulfate) per acre are generally adequate and economical.

Chelated iron products have been formulated to hold iron in an available form for a period of time. Most chelates are synthetic organic compounds that release the iron slowly. These materials are somewhat expensive, but one application can eliminate iron deficiency for an entire sod crop period.

In areas where iron chlorosis is likely, but not yet evident, iron applications can yield 4 to 5 weeks of enhanced color, increased root growth, and lower nitrogen use. In these areas, light, frequent applications of ferrous sulfate at 5 to 10 pounds of elemental iron per acre would make good management sense.

Iron can be applied dry or in a spray solution or it can be injected into the irrigation system. Ferrous sulfate dissolves readily and can be sprayed. The chelates are liquids.

If high rates of iron are applied and daily temperatures are high, the iron will burn where the spray rig's tractor tires pass. The burn usually turns the turf black. If the sprayer is behind the tires, the burn will be slight but noticeable. If the tires run over the sprayed area, the burn will be severe. Irrigation must follow immediately after application to prevent a short-term discoloration of the entire field. Iron solutions will leave a rusty color on pipe, walks, driveways, and equipment, so they should be handled carefully.

Liquid fertilizers

Many growers have used liquid fertilizers successfully, most often injecting them into the irrigation system. The primary nitrogen materials are 20 percent ammonium nitrate and 32 percent ammonium nitrate. Some complete (NPK) liquid fertilizers are also available.

The advantage to the liquid fertilizers is that the nutrients can be applied whenever the fields are irrigated, with considerable savings in labor. The plants don't care whether the fertilizer is wet or dry. The disadvantage is that irrigated fertilizers can be very difficult to monitor. Most irrigation systems require multiple injection points or some other engineering solution to ensure that the fertilizer reaches the intended field. Perhaps the biggest problem is that distribution uniformity is usually less with irrigation than with a spreader.

Pest control

Turfgrasses grown for sod usually have fewer pest problems than established turf. Disease and insect populations tend to not build up, since the turf is nearly always new and young. Fumigation effectively reduces or eradicates pests.

If a particular pest, especially a disease such as *Pythium* blight or a weed such as *Poa annua*, begins to invade a field, care should be taken to reduce its spread. Equipment should be washed before being moved between fields if the problem is a weed. For disease problems, washing with an antiseptic solution (such as diluted bleach) or steam cleaning may be necessary. Personnel should avoid walking from the infected field to a clean field without cleaning shoes or boots. This is very difficult, since it disrupts daily operations.

Some weeds escape fumigation, in particular those with very hard seed coats. Fortunately, the weeds that do escape can usually be controlled selectively if they are not allowed to grow to maturity. The biggest problem with weed control after fumigation is keeping weeds out of the clean field. Good housekeeping—keeping ditches and fencerows clean—does pay off. Floodwater, irrigation from an open ditch, and runoff into reservoirs all may contain weed seed. Any of these can be a major source of contamination.

Most turf herbicides can be used on turfgrass grown for sod. Some, however, inhibit root or rhizome development. Some pre-emergent herbicides prevent hybrid bermudagrass stolons from pegging down. When applied to a bermuda sod field, they can have very disheartening results. Applied correctly, these herbicides cause no turf management problems—they just interfere with the timely production of sod.

New herbicides enter the market with some regularity, so a list of the current materials would serve little purpose here. The best practice for a sod grower is to treat a small plot and observe the effects on the crop. Educational meetings sponsored by the agricultural colleges, trade organizations, and chemical companies are valuable sources of information on pest control and the effects of control materials. Growers should use only the materials that they are confident will both control the target pest and leave the crop unhurt.

The sod grower must be sure that all sprayers, spreaders, and seeders are calibrated. If a material is applied at too low a rate, it may not do the job, wasting time and money. If applied at too high a rate, the results could be disastrous, and would certainly be costly.

Any turf disease that is a local problem can occur in a sod field. Most pathogens build up in the debris in thatch. Under normal conditions, sod crops have little of this debris, and pathogens have little opportunity to increase. Unfortunately, *Pythium* blight, southern blight, spring deadspot, and other diseases can still devastate sod fields.

The diseases that occur frequently in sod production are *Fusarium* blight, sod roll decline (SRD), and postharvest decline (PHD). All occur in hot weather and can be expected to show up from July through September.

Fusarium blight (also known as *Fusarium* blight syndrome, necrotic ring spot, and SOD disease) is very destructive to Kentucky bluegrass. The primary symptoms are circular straw-colored patches 6 to 12 inches in diameter. In severe infestations, the patches grow together and form large, irregular shapes. In some areas of the U.S., the circular patches are more like round bands with live turf in the middle, forming what is called a frog eye. The dead leaf sheaths of infected plants can be peeled away, and a dark-colored hard rot will be seen in the crown.

A couple of fungicides are labeled for *Fusarium* blight, but chemical control is far from 100 percent effective. The disease probably infects the plants sometime in the winter or early spring, destroying the roots. With any stress in hot weather, the plants die. The plants try to survive by sending out new roots above the diseased crown. These roots are very shallow, so careful irrigation during the hot months can help the turf.

A sod field damaged with *Fusarium* blight recovers very slowly. One solution is to scalp the turf and overseed with perennial ryegrass. Marketable sod can then be available in 30 to 60 days. The consumer will have no problem with the disease on the resulting Kentucky bluegrass/perennial ryegrass sod.

Sod roll decline (SRD) primarily affects cool season grasses. No symptoms can be observed in the field prior to harvest, but during the few hours between harvest and installation, the rolled or folded sod turns black and greasy looking.

Pythium spp. and *Rhizoctonia* spp. are probably the pathogens that cause SRD. Control is easy—just spray the turf 1 or 2 days before harvest with any fungicide that is labeled for the two pathogens. Timing is critical. If the turf is sprayed more than 3 days before harvest, the disease will run rampant.

Postharvest decline affects tall fescue. The turf looks just fine in the field and at installation. Then, a few days later, the turf thins out. This disease problem does not occur every year. It appears to be related to high humidity and hot temperatures, and cultural practices may contribute to its incidence. No pathogen has been identified.

Grubs, cutworms, and armyworms are the main insect pests of sod. On occasion, sod webworm has caused problems. None of these pests seems to do much harm to sod in the field, but all can cause problems for the consumer. A large group of birds working in a field is a good indicator that some kind of worm is in the sod. Any irrigation pipe laying on the turf can be moved to show worms underneath. Once identified, the worms are not difficult to control with an insecticide labeled for the specific insect.

6

Sod Harvest

Eucre Sod

Eucre Sod has a preharvest program for mature fields. Using current sales as a guide, the production staff predicts which fields must be ready for harvest within the next month. Those fields are mowed only with the reel mower. The mowing frequency increases to reduce the potential for scalping. Santa Ana bermudagrass is mowed every 2 days and Elite tall fescue is mowed every 3 days. If the temperatures are cool and the Santa Ana is not growing fast enough to recover quickly from scalping, the mowing height is raised ⅛ inch. Nitrogen fertilizer may be applied within the month, but only if the grass starts to lose color. Even then, no fertilizer is applied within 2 weeks of harvest—if color needs enhancement, iron is applied. The staff prefers that nothing be applied after the beginning of the week before harvest. They don't want to take any chance of burning the grass too late for it to recover for harvest.

When the Eucre Sod staff perceives that a field is ready for harvest, a few rolls are cut with the harvester just to make sure that the sod is ready to be lifted, even if the sod is on netting. That is the final test before harvest.

During harvest, the Eucre Sod crew works in the Elite field before moving to the Santa Ana. This is to prevent contamination of the tall fescue with bermuda. Fescue is unlikely to contaminate bermudagrass at this stage.

After a day's harvest is finished, the next 2 or 3 acres in the field are mowed and swept. The area is then irrigated for 1 hour so the soil moisture will be right the following day. If the tall fescue is not mowed, as sometimes happens when things are very busy, a small walk-behind rotary mower is used just in front of the harvester for final grooming. If a field (especially in the bermudagrass) is a little rough, the field is rolled with the flat roller.

After harvesting is finished for the day, the harvest crew washes the machine, checks for loose bolts, failed bearings, and chain condition, greases the bearings, and changes the blade. The mechanic completes any needed repairs during the night.

First thing in the morning, the crew picks up the pallet tags for the day's cut. Throughout the morning, additional orders to be cut that day are taken to the sod harvest crew. The sod is stacked onto pallets that are left in the field. Every hour or so on hot days the pallets are hosed down.

Trucks that have been delivering the previous day's harvest soon return to the farm, and are loaded in the field for the next day's deliveries. Loaded trailers are hauled into the yard, where the sod is hosed down again and tarped.

Every day the scraps and ribbons are scraped off of the field and hauled to a dump site on the farm. This helps keep missed netting from interfering with soil preparation. Every couple of days the harvested area that has not already been worked is disked while soil moisture conditions are good. Only enough unworked space is left for the delivery trucks to maneuver. Eucre Sod plans to replant the Elite field within 2 weeks of harvest. The only way to do this is to disk the soil as harvest progresses so a minimum of work is needed after harvest is complete. The Santa Ana harvest area is rotary tilled and rolled every couple of days, while the soil moisture is good for working the soil.

Eucre Sod pays the two-person harvest crew $.0075 per square foot harvested. On a 504-square-foot pallet (56 rolls of 1 square yard each), the team earns $3.78. It is relatively easy to harvest six pallets per hour,

A two-person team operates a turfgrass harvester. One worker stacks the sod while the other steers the rig.

at which rate each team member earns $11.34 per hour on a 50-50 split. By harvesting 10 pallets per hour, still a realistic number, each crew member earns $18.90 per hour and the cost to Eucre Sod remains $3.78 per pallet, or ¾ cent per square foot for harvest.

Harvest at Eucre Sod seldom takes all day. When the stackers are finished with harvest, they clean the harvester and take empty pallets to the harvest field for use the next day. Then they return to the production crew at their regular hourly pay.

The ultimate objective of sod production is the harvest. All of the care and effort has been aimed at having a perfect turfgrass sward ready to be lifted and transferred to another site. It is important that nothing go wrong at this final stage.

Grooming

In preparation for harvest, field operations for the final month should focus on grooming the turf. The goal is to make the turf look like the finest lawn one can imagine. On the day of harvest, its height should be uniform, its color as dark a green as the cultivar can be, and its density good, and it should be free of weeds, diseases, and insects.

The true test of a turfgrass sod comes when the sod cutter goes into the field. If the turf holds together, it is sod. If it does not, no matter how good it looks it is not a salable product. With the introduction of netting to turfgrass culture, there is less mystery as to when the sod will be mature enough to lift.

A properly adjusted, sharp reel mower should be used on the turf for at least the last 4 or 5 mowings. On low-mowed grasses such as hybrid bermudagrass and bentgrass, there is always the risk of scalping. Very frequent mowing can help prevent this. Raising the cutting height ¼16 inch or so for the last 2 weeks provides risk insurance.

A small walk-behind mower can be used for final grooming just in front of the harvester. A reel mower should be used on the low-mowed grass and a rotary can be used on the high-mowed turf. Even though it is labor intensive, final grooming can pay off by impressing the customer with the high sod quality. Walk-behind mowers are not made to operate 60 hours a week, so even the best machine will not last very long. It is probably just as well to purchase an inexpensive mower for this use.

In the past, various sod harvester manufacturers have built prototype machines with "grooming mowers" mounted in front of the cutting head. The threat to worker safety and related liability problems have discouraged the manufacturers' release of the units.

Mowing for grooming cannot be scheduled in quite so straightforward a manner as it may seem. Sales forecasts are as reliable as weather forecasts, so no one knows exactly when a particular field will be needed for harvest. The grooming operation must anticipate needs based on the best information available.

Once harvest has started in a field, the unharvested portion must be kept in pristine condition. This continuation of the grooming process is particularly important to ensure consistent quality in the product. A given customer may receive sod on consecutive days, sometimes for installation on the same site. Product inconsistencies may stand out dramatically.

Fertilizer applications to mature sod are meant strictly to maintain or enhance color. Nitrogen fertilizers should not be used on the turf in the last week before harvest, because there is a high risk of burning the turf in the field. Inside the sod roll or folded pad, ammonia and urea fertilizers can volatilize to act almost as fumigants, killing the grass. All nitrogen fertilizers stimulate pathogens that can kill the grass plants in the short time between harvest and installation. The risk decreases with lower temperatures, but is always present.

If color needs to be spruced up, ferrous sulfate can be applied until 72 hours before harvest without injury to the sod in the roll or folded pad. It is possible to get a response to the iron in that short a time, but a week would be better. Even if color is satisfactory, an application of ferrous sulfate can often make it just a little better. There is still a significant risk of burning the turf in the field with ferrous sulfate.

Risks are inherent in applying anything but water within the last couple of weeks. If someone makes a mistake and burns or damages the turf in some way, the sod quality goes down, or worse, the product may be unsalable. Many growers are reluctant to apply any material to sod that is ready for harvest.

By the time the turf is ready for harvest, the density either is there or it is not. Not much can be done to affect it one way or another in the short term. If the density is unsatisfactory, harvest of that field should be postponed.

Obviously, the turf is not of high quality if there are weeds in it. If only a few weeds are present at the time of grooming, a hand-weeding crew can be sent through the field. The risk of injury to the turf would be very high if any herbicide were applied. Besides, it takes several weeks for a herbicide to work and for the weeds to disappear. There probably would be insufficient time for the chemical to effect control. In addition to potential problems in the field, some herbicides can inhibit the rooting of newly installed sod for 6 to 10 weeks after application to a sod field.

Diseases and insects can infest the turf at about any time. Sod growers normally do not apply fungicides or insecticides in a routine preventive program unless there is a predictable, persistent problem. The best harvest-time insurance against diseases and insects is to have a small supply of broad-spectrum pesticides on hand and the knowledge of when they should be used.

Harvest

The harvest of sod is an operation that requires the teamwork of nearly the entire staff. The order taker, dispatcher, and harvest supervisor coordinate the orders. The production people keep the turf groomed. Irrigators keep the soil moist enough for the sod harvester. Truck drivers move the sod out of the fields and those involved in soil preparation follow immediately behind the harvest, getting the field ready for re-planting. In the center of all this is the harvest crew.

Perhaps the most closely coordinated are the irrigators and the harvest crew. Irrigation management for harvest requires a great deal of flexibility from the same irrigators who are trained to keep to a schedule. There is a relatively narrow range of acceptable soil moisture with which the harvester will work efficiently.

If the field is too wet, sod will not cut cleanly and the sod harvester will have difficulty tracking straight, so the sod pads will not be uniform. Most sod harvesters have the cutting head and conveyer on one side,

The tag on a well-stacked pallet of rolled sod shows the order number and the type and quantity of sod.

usually the right side. When traction is poor, the resistance of this machinery pulls the harvester to that side. Steering the front wheels cannot overcome the drag, but the driver can do it by riding the left side brakes. This works well to get through a wet spot, but it is hard on machinery and on people if continued for very long. In a wet field, the loaded forklifts and trucks tend to get stuck and occasionally must be unloaded and pulled free.

Wet sod causes problems for the stackers because of the weight and the accumulation of mud on conveyers, rollers, and platforms. Extra-heavy sod reduces the number of pallets a truck can haul.

All of this discussion loses its relevance in the event of rain. The entrepreneurial sod grower will try to harvest in the rain if the customer will accept the grass. The soil type determines whether rainy-day harvest is possible or how long after a rain the crew must wait. In any case, damage to the field is disregarded. The harvester driver does the best job possible, given the conditions. If necessary, a tractor with cleated tires may be used to assist the harvester by pulling the unit. Four-wheel-drive forklifts with cleated tires can get the sod out of the field.

Sod harvesters are practically inoperative when the soil is dry and hard. The cutter blade bounces out of the ground, the sod has little strength if it can be cut, and the turf is often dead by the time it gets to the customer. The one benefit of hard soil is that trucks and forklifts do little damage, but this is unimportant if the sod cannot be harvested.

High temperatures and drying winds require that extra attention be paid to the irrigation. Under these conditions, keeping the soil soft enough to cut may necessitate interrupting the harvest to water the field. The exposed sod on the pallet should not be allowed to dry out, or that turf will be killed. Pallets can be watered with sprinklers or with a hose. Moving the sod pallets into shade helps reduce the heat and drying.

In fields with 2 percent slope or more, harvest should begin on the higher side. Unless the entire field can be lifted in one day, some irrigation will be needed before the field is finished, and the new water should run downhill, away from the harvest and the harvested area. The harvested area can then dry so it can be worked with soil preparation equipment before the entire field is harvested. If the harvest begins at the lower end of the field, sod will be cut in mud until the field is finished and the harvested area will stay wet.

Harvest has to run parallel to the irrigation laterals to allow for efficient harvest irrigation management. Where center pivots are used, the harvester follows the track of the towers and usually begins on the outside of the pattern, spiraling toward the center.

When opening up a field to harvest, the sod harvester has to run on turf for the first few passes. This always has the potential of rutting and damaging sod. To avoid further turf injury, the harvester should carry the loaded pallets to the end of the field most convenient for loading.

This keeps the forklift off the turf. After the harvested area is wide enough for trucks and forklifts, harvest becomes much more efficient.

Sod is cut with ½ to ⅝ inch of soil attached. If cut much thicker, it will have significant problems rooting. If cut much thinner, its moisture-holding capacity will be inadequate to keep the sod fresh until installation.

The size of the sod pad has a great deal to do with the efficiency of the harvest. With large sod pads such as 1 square yard (9 square feet), the stacker has fewer pads to handle and stacking is faster. In order to stack pads of 5 square feet as fast as the square-yard size, the smaller pads must come out of the harvester like machine-gun bullets. The market determines the size of the sod pad, but if the grower can influence the market, there is great advantage in the larger size.

In defense of smaller sod pads, they tend to waste less sod. A small hole may cause a sod pad to be thrown out, and it is less expensive to throw away 5 square feet than to reject a square yard.

The operator's manual for each harvester suggests a technique for stacking the sod on the pallet. Sod is arranged in layers such that the layers tie together. If stacked improperly, the sod will fall off the pallet during handling.

Sod harvesting machines have conveyers that carry the sod up to a rolling or folding attachment. Part of a sod pad is being drawn up the conveyer before the rest of it is severed from the field. Tender sod will only tolerate a little of this tension, and then will tear apart. With tender sod, the conveyer speed should be as close as possible to the harvester's ground speed. This can be gauged by the distance between pads as they progress up the conveyer. Spacing for normal sod might be 6 inches, but for tender sod it would be 2 inches. Harvester blades must also be changed more frequently on the tender sod.

Flat rolling tender sod will sometimes help it hold together for harvest. First the soil is irrigated with more moisture than would normally be good for harvest. Then a heavy flat roller is run across the harvest area. This technique does not work on sandy soils because the sand will not stick together like a more clayey soil.

Most grasses should be harvested without leaving ribbons or strips. If the harvest width is 18 inches and the harvester leaves a 2-inch ribbon, that amounts to a 10 percent waste. When other losses from field ends, holes, and the like are added in, the percentage lost can get very high. St. Augustinegrass and some other grasses must either regrow from ribbons or be replanted. Leaving ribbons may be less expensive than replanting, so 2-inch wide ribbons of St. Augustinegrass are generally left in the field.

Pallet tags are printed on card stock, with spaces for the order number, number of pallets in the order, volume on the pallet (e.g., square footage), number of pads, and kind of grass. Some growers color-code the paper or ink for different kinds of grass in order to reduce errors. The harvest supervisor makes out the tags and gives them to the sod stacker. The stacker puts the appropriate number of pads on the pallet, and then folds the tag and sticks one end between sod pads. The exposed end shows the information. The loader matches the order numbers to the loading sequence on the trucks and makes sure that the correct number of pallets is present for each order. Pallet tags provide a method of monitoring the orders and can serve to meet regulations in states that require labels.

Sod is perishable, and should be harvested to order. If the sod has to remain on the pallet more than 36 hours, especially in hot weather, it will deteriorate very quickly. The grower who delivers sod that has been on the pallet too long soon runs out of customers.

Harvest is one operation in a sod company that lends itself to piecework. The two workers on the harvester can be paid on a square-foot-stacked basis. The driver may receive 40 percent and the stacker 60 percent of the rate, because of the difference in work required. If the two workers are willing to switch places on a regular basis, the rate can be split 50-50.

For piecework to work in sod harvesting, the sod has to be of consistent quality. If the sod quality is poor and waste is high, the crew may have to harvest too slowly, and may lose their incentive. If the sod quality is marginal, it is likely that all sod will be stacked and none rejected. The crew may not take the time to select for quality control.

Netting left in the field

In fields where netting has been used, some will always remain after harvest. Some netting will have been planted too deep and the harvester will have cut the sod above it. Netting laid on the surface seldom lies too deep, except in ruts and depressions caused by footprints and tire tracks.

Scrap sod that has been cut and rejected should be removed from the field in any event, especially scraps that contain netting. In the worst case, a poor area such as a wet spot will have been skipped in the harvest. Unless the harvester goes back in and cuts that sod out to be discarded, the soil preparation equipment will run through it. The netting will ball up and wrap around equipment. Landplaning will be nearly impossible.

One of the big disadvantages of netting is that, if there are production problems, it must be removed from the field. It is considerably less expensive to take elaborate care during production so you can harvest all of the netted sod.

7

Distribution

Eucre Sod

Eucre Sod adds no delivery charge for orders of 1,000 square feet or more. In a zone between 40 and 60 miles of the farm the sod price is increased by 1 cent per square foot to help cover delivery costs. For deliveries over 60 miles distant, the price is quoted on an individual basis considering volume and distance. Orders between 500 and 1,000 square feet also carry an additional delivery charge of $20. The company will not deliver orders of less than 500 square feet.

Since there are occasions when a customer needs less than 500 square feet of sod, Eucre Sod offers will-call pick up of sod. This is useful for landscapers who have underestimated and need a little sod to complete a job or for those who simply have a small job. An occasional retail sale is made will-call, but Eucre Sod does not pursue retail sales in order to keep from competing with its nursery customers.

Eucre Sod employs two delivery truck drivers. Both are good company representatives who get along very well with the customers and, usually, with the dispatcher. The drivers wear uniforms with the company logo, so they are usually neat and clean. They receive monthly bonuses of $75 each if their tractors and trailers pass the general manager's weekly inspection. The inspection simply confirms that the service is current (oil and lubrication), the lights work, the brakes are adjusted, the vehicle has been washed, and the cab is clean and neat.

Normally, sod is loaded onto trucks in the field. On rainy days or on hot, windy days, the sod is sometimes taken out of the field to be loaded onto the trucks later. Eucre Sod trucks usually haul up to 18 pallets on each trailer.

Eucre Sod has two three-axle tractors and four 40-foot trailers. The extra two trailers can be loaded and waiting for the drivers to return and make two runs each per day. A totable forklift rides on the back of each trailer on delivery runs.

A typical delivery run begins when driver Jerry Rigg returns the empty truck to the farm after a day's run. He stops by the office to drop off the paperwork and discuss the day's events over a cup of coffee. Jerry picks up the load sheet showing the order the pallets are to be loaded onto his trailer for the next day's deliveries. The first delivery is on the back of the trailer and the last delivery is on the front. He has 18 pallets to go to four drop-sites.

Jerry takes his truck into the field where the pallets are waiting. He uses the field forklift loading, since it has side-shift on the mast for faster and tighter loading. The sod stackers are good and the pallets are straight and neat. Jerry can easily keep the load inside the trailer dimensions.

When the sod is loaded, Jerry slowly drives to the yard. If the dirt farm roads were too rough he would have to tarp and tie the load in the field to keep the sod from loosening and perhaps falling off. In the yard, he waters down the sod with a hose and then tarps and ties the load.

Back in the office, Jerry picks up the paperwork for the new load. The invoices show the customer name, drop-site address, nearest major cross streets, order number, number of pallets in the order, type of grass, and whether the purchase terms are open account or cash-on-delivery (COD). If the order is COD, Jerry must collect the money before leaving the sod. A COD delivery will often mean a delay in getting to the next drop. Jerry only has one COD delivery scheduled.

Jerry puts the paperwork in the truck cab. Before going home, he checks the lights and tires—now is the time to take care of those things, rather than at 5:00 A.M. when he has a load to deliver.

When Jerry arrives the next morning, he starts the big diesel engine and lets it warm up as he again checks the lights and tires of the rig. Jerry arrives at his first drop on time at 6:30 A.M. The landscaper is there and shows Jerry where he wants the four pallets placed throughout the site so they will be convenient for his crew. The landscaper signs the delivery receipt and the two of them chat while Jerry puts the forklift back on the trailer and reties the load.

Still on time, Jerry arrives at the second drop at 7:30 A.M. To get to where this landscaper wants his six pallets placed, Jerry must cross a new driveway with concrete that is still green. Jerry knows that the heavy sod and forklift could crack the driveway. He and the landscaper agree on an alternate route that will take much more time. When he is finally ready to leave, Jerry calls the office on the two-way radio and tells the dispatcher what has happened, and that he is now about ½ hour late.

The next delivery is COD and Jerry arrives at 9:15 A.M., ½ hour late. There is no one around. Jerry calls the office on the radio and asks what he should do. The dispatcher calls the landscaper's office, but there is no answer. The dispatcher then uses the radio to call Steve Zapatas, the sales representative, to see if he can help. Steve knows where the landscaper drinks coffee in the morning and agrees to see if he can find him. An hour later, Steve and the landscaper show up. Jerry gets the check for the sod, places the two pallets for the landscaper, and gets back on the road. He is now nearly 2 hours late.

The last drop was scheduled for 10:30 A.M. It is now 11:30 A.M. and Jerry is still an hour away from the site. This landscaper was called and informed that the truck was about 2 hours late, but he is understandably upset because his crew has been standing around drawing wages. When Jerry arrives, Steve is already on the site and the landscaper is well into a tirade against the company. The two Eucre Sod employees let the landscaper blow off the steam that has built up over the late delivery. Since this is the last delivery of the day, Jerry offers to help with installation by staying on site and moving the pallets as the crew works. That way they will not have to walk so far. It takes less than an hour to lay the six pallets of sod. When Jerry and Steve leave, the landscaper is happy and thanks them for the help. Jerry returns to the farm to get ready for the next day's run.

Installation problems are serviced by Steve Zapatas. Steve can often prevent a small problem from becoming a big one by visiting the delivery site during installation. Visiting all the sites is impossible, but Steve tries to stop by all of the big jobs well as some of the smaller ones. When complaints are called in, Steve is contacted over the two-way radio in his car. He makes a service call as soon as is practical.

Sod distribution

Service can be defined as getting the sod product to the customer fresh and in a timely manner. It is the single most important marketing tool a sod grower has. All of the hard work and care that goes into growing turf means little to the customer. What comes across is service.

After the sod is harvested, some customers may pick up their own orders. The volume of will-call business depends somewhat on the location of the farm, but more on the desire of the sod company to encourage it. Will-call has its own service demands, requiring that employees be free to serve customers who may be wandering around the operation. This can be an important market segment for some growers.

Most sod is delivered, so the people most often seen by customers are the delivery personnel. The truck drivers and their equipment provide an image of the company. They *are* the company in the eyes of the customer. Well-maintained, clean equipment indicates a classy operation. A friendly, cooperative driver can and will contribute to future sales. Some growers rent uniforms for their drivers from a laundry service in order to project an image of orderliness and to make the drivers feel more a part of the company.

Customers order the sod because they are ready to use it, regardless of which sod company they call. On the day of delivery, they expect the truck to show up on time. Often they have people standing around drawing wages, waiting to lay sod. An occasional late delivery will be tolerated, but repeated problems will send the customer to look for another supplier.

Equipment breakdowns and flat tires are the most frequent reasons for late deliveries. Good maintenance helps control these problems but does not eliminate them.

Dispatching and routing are also prime causes of late deliveries. The dispatcher must know the delivery area and the time required to unload and travel between customers. It is quite important that the order takers, dispatcher, and truck drivers work as a team.

Weight

Sod is heavy. Grown on mineral soil, it weighs about 5 pounds per square foot, depending upon the thickness of the cut and the amount of moisture retained. A pallet with 500 square feet on it will weigh about 2,500 pounds. That is about all a half-ton pickup truck can carry and more than one would wish to load into an automobile. Delivery trucks must be strong, sturdy vehicles.

Sod grown on muck soils is much lighter, and a truck can haul 25 to 30 percent more muck sod than mineral sod. Muck soils, organically formed from old bogs, are found in many parts of the U.S., but most of the nation's sod grows on mineral soil.

Each state has laws governing the amount of weight each axle of a truck can carry over the road. In most states, a three-axle tractor with a trailer 40 feet long and a forklift can carry no more than 18 pallets with 500 square feet of sod each, because of the weight.

Loading

Pallets are loaded onto the truck according to the delivery routing. The last pallet to be delivered will go on the truck first. Since the truck or trailer bed is 8 feet wide and the pallets are 4 feet square, two should easily go on side by side. If the sod is not stacked correctly, a pallet may be a little bigger than it should be. In that case, two pallets side by side will be wider than 8 feet and the load will be subject to overwidth penalties. Regulatory authorities tend to be inflexible when it comes to load weight, length, and width. Sod delivery vehicles normally have no trouble with load height regulations.

Sod is either loaded directly onto delivery trucks in the field or hauled to a distribution yard. There, the pallets are arranged by order number, held until all trucks are ready, and then loaded onto the delivery trucks.

Since the soil in the harvest field is moist enough for harvest, loading sod trucks in the soft field causes compaction and rutting. A muddy field compounds the damage. In muddy conditions, the pallets should be taken to the end of the field either by the harvester or a forklift and then loaded onto the truck.

If the sod pallets are to sit for any period of time, they should be watered down to prevent the outside edges from drying. Some growers have built shade covers with sprinklers for their holding areas. This helps keep the sod cool and the outside sod pieces moist. Hose connections can be put on sprinkler pipe to water pallets of sod left in the field for loading.

After the sod is loaded, the driver should tarp and tie the load with ropes. The tarp will both prevent the sod from drying out and keep it on the pallet during the ride.

Distribution equipment

Delivery systems vary with each grower. The most common delivery vehicles are a three-axle tractor with a trailer 40 feet long, a two-axle tractor with two trailers 24 and 26 feet long, and a three-axle truck with a 24-foot bed pulling a 26-foot trailer.

Delivery forklifts are either totable, and carried as part of the load, or towable, and towed behind the rig. As you might expect, there are advantages and disadvantages to each. Every grower either thinks his or her system is the best, or swallows his or her pride and switches to a better one.

A three-axle tractor with a 40-foot trailer has one hinge point, the pivoting point for the trailer, and can either tow or tote a forklift. With a towable lift unhooked, this rig can back easily into a job site. It also has only 18 tires as potential flats, not counting the forklift tires. The disadvantage is that the rig cannot turn sharply and can haul only 18 pallets (20 if the sod is light).

A towable forklift ready to load pallets onto the delivery truck.

A two-axle tractor with double trailers can haul 24 pallets and turn around in a cul-de-sac. However, the rig has 22 tires as potential flats and it cannot be backed up. Moreover, with two hinge points (where the first trailer pivots on the tractor and the second trailer pivots on the first), it cannot by law use a towable lift. The delivery forklift has to be totable.

The truck and trailer combination is a favorite with small growers as it offers the opportunity to make small deliveries without the trailer or to haul 24 pallets with the trailer, and can use either a towable or a totable lift. With the trailer hooked up, the rig is difficult to back up and has a fairly wide turning radius.

Towable forklifts are quite heavy—around 9,000 pounds—to counterbalance the weight of the loaded pallet. They offer a narrow wheel base, which can often be useful in reaching areas through narrow gates or openings. If the truck cannot get close to the delivery site, this type of lift has a fast transport time running back and forth from the truck to the job site, and is usually better than a totable for climbing hills.

This totable forklift easily hoists itself onto the back of the delivery truck.

The disadvantages are that towable forklifts are usually more expensive, put four more tires on the road, and take a tremendously severe beating in daily use just being towed over the road. If the driver ever fails to take the lift out of gear after hooking it up to the truck, the lift's engine and transmission will be destroyed within a few miles. Repair usually costs several thousand dollars. Towing in gear is a major problem, no matter what the forklift sales representative may say.

Totable lifts are much lighter than towables. They lift the load by straddling the pallet rather than counterweighting it. The forks also fit into a set of pockets on the back of a trailer or truck and, with a two-way hydraulic ram, the lift will hoist itself off of the ground. Safety chains or cables are then attached and the forklift becomes part of the trailer or truck. Totables are usually cheaper to buy and maintain than towables. Because the unit wraps around the pallet, a totable has a short turning radius, but its extra width will keep it from getting through many narrow openings such as backyard gates. Totables tend to be slow in transporting over distances and are underpowered on hills.

Field forklifts are not normally adapted for use in deliveries. These lifts have mud-grip tires and many have four-wheel drive. A grower needs this type of lift to be able to get the sod out of the field in marginal weather. The sod farm should be capable of harvesting and delivering sod any time a customer can receive it. There are times, though, when delivery is impossible.

Some markets have accepted the curbside delivery, rather than demanding that pallets be placed for the convenience of the customer. In these areas, many trucks or trailers carry permanently mounted booms that simply set each pallet off of the vehicle.

Tarps to reduce moisture loss should be long enough to cover the full length of the maximum load and reach the deck from the top of the average pallet. They should be wide enough to go from the deck, over the pallets, and to the deck on the other side. For a 40-foot trailer, the tarp would be about 48 feet by 16 feet. The tarp should be made out of the lightest, most durable material available, and even at that it can weigh a couple of hundred pounds. It is good to keep in mind that the driver must wrestle the tarp around, often in the wind. A light colored tarp shows dirt readily, but helps reduce heat buildup inside the load.

Sod pallets are actually called "skids" in the pallet industry, because boards are only on the top of the stringers. A common specification for a sod pallet is 48 inches square, with three 2x4s as stringers and five 1x6s on the top, and with 4-inch wings (overhanging beyond the outside stringers). Sod pallets are normally made from the cheapest lumber available, since few are returned. The handling of pallets is one of the many headaches a sod grower has to deal with.

Distribution is where a company can nearly always outperform its competition. Here the service image is built.

On the job site

Troubleshooting turfgrass sod after it has been installed can be a mind-boggling process. The sod grower does have some responsibility for the turf for the first month or so after delivery, but not the only responsibility.

Sod pads with one dead end or with dead edges indicate that the sod got too dry before installation. The ends and edges were at the outside of the pallet. This could be the responsibility of the grower or the installer. One or the other let the sod dry out.

Weeds within sod pads are the responsibility of the sod grower. Weeds growing in the seams between sod pads are the fault of the installer. If the sod pads butt tightly against each other, weeds seldom grow in the seams.

Irrigation patterns on the job site cause frequent complaints of defective sod. It is easy to tell whether the pattern fits the irrigation system on the site. If the dead sod pads cluster in groups around a sprinkler head, the fault probably does not belong with the grower. Also, professional installers tend to work within 30 or 40 feet of a pallet, so if part or all of a pallet of sod were bad, the sod would probably not be spread throughout the site.

It is sometimes handy to remember that sod is harvested in rows, so each pallet holds a long, narrow strip of a field. If there were a bad spot in the field, it would probably appear on several pallets and more than one customer would be likely to receive the same bad turf.

Sod that does not root may be suffering from some type of soil contamination. It can be very difficult to tell whether something was poured on the soil or buried before installation. Herbicides cannot automatically be ruled out. Some cause distinctive symptoms on the turf, such as white blade tips or yellow streaks. Household bleach, gasoline, and other common chemicals can cause injuries similar to those caused by herbicides. The grower could also be at fault for having applied herbicides to the field, but usually these materials do not cause foliar symptoms. The sod thickness should be checked, since sod that is cut too thick roots very slowly. Where sod grown on a heavy clay soil is laid on a sandy soil or where sandy sod is laid on clay soil, the sod may not root through the sod-to-soil interface.

If the sod is not watered well at installation, rooting can be very slow. The sod should be watered sufficiently to soak through the sod piece and wet the soil underneath. Sod installed on slopes is very hard to water correctly. Once it is rooted, it is only as difficult to maintain on the slope as any other turf would be.

Insects found in the sod during the first 30 days could be the responsibility of the grower. After that, they will usually have come from a source on or close to the site.

Appendix

Equipment

Eucre Sod

The equipment owned by Eucre Sod (table 10) is typical of that needed on a 100- to 200-acre sod farm. Eucre Sod has a 130 horsepower tractor. The disk is a 12-foot offset unit of medium weight, with 22-inch blades. The cultipacker is 12 feet wide and the landplane is 40 feet long with a 12-foot bucket. The plow is a four-bottom, 18-inch moldboard that flips over for consecutive return passes. The rotary tiller is an 8-foot unit that requires all of the horsepower of the big tractor.

Both utility tractors at Eucre Sod are 50-horsepower units, and one has a quick-detachable loader. A 6-foot-wide tilting scraper blade was purchased, and a local welding shop built a 4-foot-diameter, 8-foot-wide split flat roller.

Eucre Sod has a three-point-hitch-mount broadcast spreader with a 1-ton capacity. This will apply 500 pounds of ammonium sulfate (21-0-0) per acre to 4 acres with one filling. The trailer-mounted sprayer has a

Table 10. Eucre Sod equipment list

Description	Estimated cost	Description	Estimated cost
Tractor: 130 hp min.	$ 70,000	Brought forward	$279,000
Flipover moldboard plow: 4 bottom	20,000	Seeder: 8'	3,000
Disk: 12'	15,000	2 sweeper/vacuums: 10'	15,000
Cultipacker: 12'	15,000	Flat roller: 8'	2,500
Rotary tiller: 8'	18,000	Sod harvester	35,000
Landplane: 40' x 12'	20,000	Field forklift	25,000
Tractor w/ turf tires: 50 hp	15,000	2 delivery trucks/trailers	150,000
Tractor w/ turf tires: 50 hp, loader	18,000	2 delivery forklifts	44,000
Sprayer: 400 gal., 25' boom	3,500	Solid-set irrigation	55,000
Broadcast spreader	2,000	5 wheel lines	25,000
Reel mower: 16' (7 gang, 4-blade reels)	30,000	Mainlines	150,000
Reel mower: 12' (5 gang, 6-blade reels)	21,000	2 pipe trailers	4,000
Rotary mower: 16'	28,000	Office equipment	3,500
Flail mower: 16'	3,500	Maintenance shop equipment	5,000
Carried forward	279,000	Total equipment cost	$796,000

400-gallon fiberglass tank, mechanical agitation, a PTO driven pump capable of producing 60 psi, and a 25-foot boom. The seeder is 8 feet wide and drops the seed between two rows of ring rollers similar to the rings of a cultipacker.

The Eucre Sod mower fleet includes a seven-gang self-propelled mower and a five-gang self-propelled mower, each with hydraulically driven reels; a 16-foot-wide rotary mower; and an 8-foot-wide three-point-hitch-mount flail. The smaller reel mower is for mowing bermudagrass and has 6-blade reels, unlike the 4-blade reels of the larger mower. Two sweeper/vacuums with 10-foot swaths are also in the inventory.

To harvest the sod, Eucre Sod has a sod harvester with rolling attachment. The harvested sod is 18 inches wide by 72 inches long (1 square yard). The harvester is the simplest made, with no extras.

The Eucre Sod water source is a well pumped at 3,000 gallons per minute (gpm) and 55 psi, with no quality problems. Eucre Sod owns 2,000 feet of 8-inch, and 1,320 feet of 6-inch aluminum aboveground portable mainline. There are 50 joints of 8-inch pipe and 33 joints of 6-inch pipe 40 feet long with a 4-inch valve on each joint.

The fields are divided into convenient quarter-mile lengths which will make each bay (the area between the irrigation laterals) 1.2 acres ([1,320 feet x 40 feet]/43,560 square feet). Eucre Sod has approximately 50 acres' supply of 3-inch solid-set laterals—42 sets of 44 joints 30 feet long, for a total of 1,848 joints (44 joints x 42 laterals). There are 1,848 sprinklers with $^{11}\!/_{64}$-inch nozzles, and 42 endplugs. That essentially, is a 50-acre solid-set sod production system, capable of covering one-half of the Eucre Sod tall fescue acreage.

Obviously, grass grows on the other 50 acres plus the 10 acres of Santa Ana. In normal production, some land is in preparation, some is newly planted, some is approaching maturity, and some is in harvest. The newly planted turf is irrigated with the solid set. All of the rest is irrigated by movable wheel lines.

The Eucre Sod wheel lines are made up of 4-inch-diameter by 40-foot-long aluminum pipe on 52-inch diameter wheels, with a powered mover. With this configuration, as the wheels move, the sprinklers turn fully over three times between valves, and all stop upright for the next valve. Each lateral has 32 of these joints with ¼-inch sprinklers, and a gasoline-powered mover is placed in the center of each wheel line.

Each quarter-mile wheel line is expected to irrigate approximately 10 acres of turf. Since there is always some land that needs no irrigating, Eucre Sod needs only four of these lines for the tall fescue and an additional one for the Santa Ana bermudagrass. Five 4- by 4-inch valve openers, five end plugs, and five hook-up hoses 20 feet long and 4 inches in diameter are also needed. A pipe trailer hauls the wheel line sections and another hauls the solid-set pipe.

Eucre Sod has two three-axle tractors, four 40-foot trailers, and two totable forklifts in its distribution fleet. The tractors are equipped with two-way radios to keep in contact with the farm dispatcher.

The Eucre Sod office equipment consists of three computers that can be networked, but are not. Invoices and billing statements are printed by a computer, as are accounting and customer records. Desks, chairs, tables, file cabinets, calculators, the radio base station, and a seldom-used typewriter make up the rest of the office equipment.

An arc welder, oxyacetylene tanks and torch, an air compressor, a battery charger, a hydraulic press, hydraulic jacks, a cut-off saw, various engine testing instruments, and several hundred pounds of hand and power tools equip the Eucre Sod maintenance shop.

Production equipment

After the land, the largest investment a sod producer must make is in equipment. The soil preparation equipment is the same as that used on any farm raising a crop that requires high-intensity management. The production equipment is much like that used on golf courses and in parks. A few of the pieces are specialized for sod production.

Land preparation equipment

A grower can contract land preparation work out or rent the equipment. As the farm develops, these operations occur often enough to require that the grower own the equipment. A powerful tractor (100 to 160 horsepower) is needed to pull the plow, disk harrow, cultipacker, and landplane. A large rotary tiller will also require a tractor with a great deal of power.

The tractor and implements must match for efficiency. Each pound per foot width of a disk requires a certain horsepower to pull it when working at a given depth in a given soil. Disks are commonly one of two types: tandem and offset. Each varies by weight, blade type, diameter, thickness, and overall width.

Plows, cultipackers, and other implements are also available in various forms to perform specific jobs. Sod growers who are unfamiliar with this kind of equipment may be wise to rely on the equipment dealer to match the equipment to their needs. Failing that, the coffee shop where local farmers congregate will be a fine source of information with varying degrees of reliability.

Crawler-type tractors are good for soil preparation. Their traction is excellent and the resultant compaction is minimal. Some people feel that crawlers are slower than wheeled tractors, but they still seem to get the job done. A crawler tractor with a bulldozer blade is an extremely useful tool around any farm.

Cultipackers are very simple tools that break up the clods of soil after disking. The implement consists of a series of toothed or notched cast iron rings loosely placed on a shaft; as it is pulled, the rings turn in a disjointed manner. Normally, the cultipacker is the same width as the disk and can be attached behind the disk for a one-pass operation.

A landplane is quite important to the sod grower. This unit is designed to smooth the soil. The precision of any landplane depends upon the length of the wheel base, the width of the bucket, and the skill of the operator, not necessarily in that order. Landplanes are commonly 30 to 80 feet long and as wide as the tractor can pull. The longer units are capable of more precise smoothing.

Even though landplanes appear simple to use, their proper operation requires a great deal of skill. Some landplanes use a mechanical or hydraulic linkage to add the length of the tractor to their own effective length. Some owners like these; others do not.

The newest entry into the landplane market is the laser-activated landplane, which is both very accurate and very expensive. Even if a grower normally uses a mechanical landplane, occasional use of a custom operator's laser unit will help prevent low and high spots in a field.

General equipment

The sod grower can get by at first with only one small utility tractor, but will eventually need a second. With only one, the grower will constantly be trying to catch up on needed work. Utility tractors are always in short supply on the farm. They are used to seed, fertilize, spray, mow, sweep, haul pipe, pull trailers, and perform any number of jobs around the farm. There are really too many such tasks for a single tractor to handle for long.

These tractors should have flotation tires or turf tires on front and back. Wheel weights and front "suitcase" weights are often important—some farm tractors are light in relation to their horsepower. The tractors should have power take-off (PTO), three-point hitch, and remote hydraulics.

Any equipment that you expect to drive on the turf should have some kind of flotation tires, which are wide and have a tread other than the traditional tractor tire cleats. Some are designated specifically as turf tires. Even though they reduce traction, especially on bare soil, these tires significantly reduce damage to the turf.

A front-end loader is extremely useful to the sod grower. This is used to pick up scraps and to move soil and other material. One utility tractor should have a mounted loader. Detachable loaders are available, and these can be mounted or dismounted from the tractor as needed.

A scraper or blade to mount on the rear of the tractor is almost a necessity. This can be used to maintain roads, drainage ditches, and truck loading areas.

A flat roller is made of smooth steel and looks much like the road rollers used in paving, except that on the sod farm the roller is normally pulled rather than self-propelled. It should be at least 8 feet wide. Growers vary in their preference of roller diameter, but 4 feet is a popular dimension. Many flat rollers are split in the center, to make turning easier. An 8-foot roller that is not split will tear turf when making turns. The roller should have the option of being filled with water so the operator can add additional weight as needed. Flat rollers are not widely available in the marketplace, so you may need to have one built at a local welding shop.

The soil may need rolling just before seeding if clods have not broken up. Sod sometimes needs rolling as it nears harvest to smooth the field for the harvester.

Applicators

A fertilizer spreader is necessary to a sod operation. Two types are common on sod farms: drop spreaders and broadcast spreaders. A drop spreader has a box across the width of the unit to hold the fertilizer. The fertilizer drops straight down onto the soil. These applicators are very accurate when in good repair.

A broadcast spreader has a hopper that holds the fertilizer and drops it onto a spinning impeller. The fertilizer is thrown across a wide swath. Broadcast spreaders are not as accurate as drop spreaders, but they are considerably faster and an inexperienced operator is less likely to skip spots.

The sod farm will need a good sprayer. Sprayer tanks should be made of either stainless steel or fiberglass, since agricultural chemicals are corrosive. Some sort of agitation is needed to keep the chemicals in the tank in suspension. Mechanical agitation, where a paddle or impeller in the tank is powered by the same power source as drives the pump, is preferable. Bypass agitation is another common method that requires no additional belts, pulleys, bearings, seals, or holes in the tank. A stream is split from the application solution after it leaves the pump, and that stream is forced turbulently back into the tank.

The application pressure of a sprayer used on a sod farm seldom has to exceed 60 pounds per square inch, so a centrifugal pump will work efficiently. Pumps are powered by the tractor PTO or a mounted gasoline engine. Both work well, but farmers tend to have better success maintaining PTO units than small engines. Spray boom width should be matched to the needs of the farm. This depends upon the distance between the irrigation laterals, among other factors.

Planters

No sod farm can get along without a seeder. The seeder should be at least 8 feet wide. Several very efficient, low-maintenance seeders are on the market.

Most seeders work by dropping seed through slots onto measuring flutes. The seed falls from the flutes onto a baffle that spreads the stream of seed, and then drops to the soil between two sets of ring rollers or disk blades. The ring rollers are similar to cultipacker rings. The front rollers dibble the soil, and the rear rollers lightly cover the seed. Seeders with disk blades work in a similar way. These two types of seeder have been in use since the 1920s and may need little improvement for many years to come.

Mowers

Reel mowers are the elite of turf-cutting units. As the reel turns, it forces the grass blades against the bedknife like one scissors blade forcing a piece of paper against the other. The reel-to-bedknife relationship is precisely adjusted. It is easy and very expensive to ruin a reel. Sharpening should be done by a professional.

In backlapping, the reel turns backward while a fine abrasive grit is applied. This grinds against the bedknife, removing minute amounts of steel from both bedknife and reel. Backlapping serves to seat the reel to the bedknife, and to remove some nicks from and sharpen both. At some point, the reel will need to be ground on a machine and the bedknife either sharpened or replaced.

Backlapping can be done in the farm shop. A mower should be back-lapped more or less frequently depending upon the type of grass mowed and how much soil goes through the reels. Ryegrass and bermudagrass dull mowers rather quickly. A rule of thumb is to backlap after 50 to 75 hours of operation. Mowers with reels are that driven independently of the wheels can usually be reversed by opening a valve on the hydraulic system or by reversing a drive belt. Those that are driven by the wheels require a backlapping kit and motor attachment to run backwards.

The warm season grasses grown as fine turf require reel mowing, primarily because of the low cutting height. Reels that are driven hydraulically or by mechanical linkage to the power unit rather than ground drive are preferable because they have consistent cutting power. The wheels on ground-drive units tend to slip, decreasing the power to the reels.

As the reels turn, the mower moves over the ground. The time that elapses while the reel gathers grass blades into the bedknife for cutting determines the *clip rate* of the reel. The clip rate must be quicker for low-mowed grasses than for those mowed high. If the clip rate is too slow for a grass, the cut will not be uniform. Parallel ridges (*marcels*) will mark the turf.

The clip rate of a reel mower corresponds to the number of times a reel blade crosses the bedknife in relation to the forward speed of the mower. It can be increased by increasing the revolutions per minute of the reel, by increasing the number of blades on the reel, or by slowing the forward speed of the mower.

Kentucky bluegrass mowed at 1½ inches can be mowed with a four-blade reel. Bermudagrass mowed at ⅝ inch must have a six-blade reel at least. Bentgrass on a golf green mowed at 3/32 inch has to have an 11-blade, high-speed reel. Bluegrass can be mowed with a six-blade reel with no problem, but an 11-blade reel creates so much turbulent air that the long grass blades are blown aside. The reel mower you select will depend on your intended use.

The first few mowings of stolonized grasses are hard on reels and bedknives because of extensive contact with soil. A flail may be useful for these mowings because maintenance costs are lower. The flail blades can be sharpened in the farm shop. If they need to be replaced, the cost is less than that of sharpening reels and bedknives. In the spring, when the grasses are coming out of dormancy, a flail mower will cut the old leaf material, opening the way for new growth.

Most cool season grasses can be mowed readily with rotary or flail mowers. Rotary mowers are available in widths up to 16 feet for large operations and can be efficient time savers. They usually cost less to maintain than reel mowers.

A flail mower does not have the high blade-tip speed of a rotary and does not give an aesthetically pleasing cut on cool season grasses, especially ryegrasses. However, when a grower gets behind in mowing, flail mowers are handy for catching up. Just stick a flail mower on the back of a small tractor and go.

Sweepers and vacuums

In areas where crop maturity time is short, picking up the clippings will significantly improve sod quality. This operation can easily become a bottleneck. Vacuum and sweeper equipment is not widely available in sizes as wide as mowers, although at least one sweeper comes close, and travel speeds are slower than for mowers. In addition, the clippings must be transported from the field when the unit is full. A large amount of clippings and a long unloading trip make for a very slow operation.

Each vacuum or sweeper needs a tractor to pull it, and few are made for the 2,000 to 3,000 annual hours of operation common on a sod farm. Equipment breaks down frequently and its useful life is short.

No simple solution has yet been developed for the clippings problem. A number of growers have built large mowers with clipping collection attachments, but none has been developed for manufacture. If the local sod market will accept the turf quality that comes without picking up clippings, the grower need not invest in this equipment.

Irrigation equipment

Irrigation systems and methods vary a great deal from one sod grower to the next. In the industry, irrigation systems range from 2-inch pipes with nozzles smaller than ⅛ inch on up to huge center pivots with nozzles big enough to hold a broom handle. The key is to apply enough water uniformly to the turf when the grass plants need it.

If the grower has the opportunity to start from scratch, then it pays to invest in the services of an irrigation consultant before purchasing equipment that might cause problems later. Most often, a grower has to figure out how to utilize facilities already in existence, such as wells, pumps, reservoirs, mainlines, and valves.

The type of soil on the land, the soil chemical analysis, the slope, the frequency, amplitude, and direction of prevailing winds, the temperature range, the available quantity and quality of water, and the kind of grasses to be grown determine the parameters of an irrigation system. Water management is complex and vital to the success of a sod operation. To operate with inappropriate irrigation equipment is to invite red ink on the year-end financial statement.

The sod harvester

Perhaps the most important piece of equipment on the sod farm, after the telephone, is the sod harvester. There are several on the market and some are quite sophisticated. All will eventually break down, and since keeping a backup unit on hand is generally too expensive for the small grower, the availability of replacement parts must enter into the purchase decision.

The cutting unit of a harvester consists of a reciprocating blade below the soil surface that severs uniform strips of sod. A vertical blade actuated by a wheel or roller running on the turf surface chops the sod strips into uniform lengths.

The simplest machines merely cut the sod, and some are capable of rolling the sod. Otherwise, laborers roll or fold the sod by hand. Either way, laborers must next pick up the sod rolls where they are left in the field and stack them on pallets. This is labor-intensive work, but this type of harvesting machine is the least expensive.

More complex harvesters cut the sod and transport it up a conveyer to a mechanical rolling or folding unit, where a laborer catches the sod and drops it onto a pallet. The least sophisticated of these harvesters requires a driver and a stacker. Some machines stack the sod mechanically and require only a driver.

Shop equipment

Just like any farm, a sod operation needs a good, well-equipped shop. There is no way to get along without welders, compressors, battery chargers, drills, saws, tire tools, pneumatic wrenches, hand tools, and the like. If there is no shop already on site, the new grower must include this structure and the tools in the budget.

Selected Bibliography

Compendium of Turfgrass Diseases, R. W. Smiley, American Phytopathological Society, St. Paul, Minn. 1983.

Diseases of Turfgrass, H. B. Couch, Robert E. Krieger Publishing Company, Inc., Huntington, N.Y. 1973.

Growers Weed Identification Handbook, Publication 4030, ANR Publications, University of California, Oakland, Calif. rev. 1987.

Guide to Turfgrass Pest Control, Publication 2209, ANR Publications, University of California, Oakland, Calif. rev. 1981.

Irrigation Costs, Publication 2875, ANR Publications, University of California, Oakland, Calif. rev. 1981.

Irrigation Technical Manual: Engineering Data, A. C. Sarsfield, Irrigation Technical Services, Publications Division, Lafayette, Calif. 1983.

Managing and Modifying Problem Soils, Publication 2791, ANR Publications, Univerity of California, Oakland, Calif. rev. 1974.

Pesticide Application and Safety Training Manual, Publication 4070, ANR Publications, University of California, Oakland, Calif. rev. 1983.

Pumping Energy Requirments in California, Publication 3215, ANR Publications, University of California, Oakland, Calif. rev. 1978.

Selective Chemical Weed Control, Publication 1919, ANR Publications, University of California, Oakland, Calif. rev. 1987.

Sprinkler Irrigation, C. H. Pair, W. W. Hinz, C. Reid, and K. R. Frost, Sprinkler Irrigation Association, Washington, D.C. rev. 1980.

Turfgrass Disease Control Guide, Publication 2619, ANR Publications, University of California, Oakland, Calif. rev. 1981.

Turfgrass Management, A. J. Turgeon, Reston Publishing Company, Inc., Reston, Va. rev. 1987.

Turfgrass Pests, Publication 4053, ANR Publications, University of California, Oakland, Calif. 1980.

Turfgrass Science: Agronomy Monograph No. 14, A. A. Hanson and F. V. Juska eds., American Society of Agronomy, Madison, Wisc. 1969.

Turfgrass Science and Culture, J. B. Beard, Prentice-Hall, Inc., Englewood Cliffs, N.J. 1973.

Turfgrass Water Conservation, Publication 21405, ANR Pubications, University of California, Oakland, Calif. 1985.

Water Wells and Pumps: Their Design, Construction, Operation, and Maintenance, Publication 1889, ANR Publications, University of California, Oakland, Calif. 1978.